PETERSON'S

Game Plan for
Getting
into
College

K. Patricia Aviezer

THOMSON

PETERSON'S

Australia • Canada • Mexico • Singapore • Spain • United Kingdom • United States

About The Thomson Corporation and Peterson's

The Thomson Corporation, with 2002 revenues of US$7.8 billion, is a global leader in providing integrated information solutions to business and professional customers. The Corporation's common shares are listed on the Toronto and New York stock exchanges (TSX: TOC; NYSE: TOC). Its learning businesses and brands serve the needs of individuals, learning institutions, corporations, and government agencies with products and services for both traditional and distributed learning. Peterson's (www.petersons.com) is a leading provider of education information and advice, with books and online resources focusing on education search, test preparation, and financial aid. Its Web site offers searchable databases and interactive tools for contacting educational institutions, online practice tests and instruction, and planning tools for securing financial aid. Peterson's serves 110 million education consumers annually.

Thanks to Richard Flaherty, College Parents of America

Visit Peterson's Education Center on the Internet (World Wide Web) at www.petersons.com

Library of Congress Cataloging-in-Publication Data

Aviezer, K. Patricia.
    Game plan for getting into college/K. Patricia Aviezer.
       p. cm.
    Summary: Explains what students should do in the years leading up to college and emphasizes critical areas of the college selection and applications process, including picking a college, applying, and paying college tuition.
    ISBN 0-7689-0390-4
      1. Universities and colleges—United States—Admission—Juvenile literature.
2. College choice—United States—Juvenile literature. [1. Universities and colleges—Admission. 2. College choice.] I. Title.

LB2351.2 .A85 2000
378.1'61—dc21   99-088974

Printed in Canada

10 9 8 7 6 5 4 3

Contents

If I'm So Smart, Why Is This So Complicated?

Chapter 1

Every spring, thousands of high school seniors across the country rush home from school and tear through the family mail with sweaty palms and pounding hearts. No, they're not searching for a $100,000 sweepstakes check. They're hoping for something far more valuable—a thick envelope from a college admissions office. High school seniors know from students who have ripped open envelopes in springs past that bad news travels "light" and good news arrives "heavy." In other words, if a college rejects you, it sends a one-page "thanks anyway" letter. But if you are accepted, you'll receive a congratulatory letter along with several pages of enrollment information—that thick envelope.

How do college admissions counselors determine whether your envelope is thick or thin? How can you learn what's important and what a college is really looking for in a prospective student? It is difficult to generalize about a process that involves more than 3,500 institutions of higher education and hundreds of thousands of students, no two of whom share the exact same academic personal profile. However, as a rule admissions counselors carefully examine six factors for each applicant. Keep in mind that in reviewing these six factors, admissions counselors look less for well-rounded students and more for students who stand out in some uniquely personal way. We'll talk more about that later in this chapter. The following are the six factors:

1. **Academic Performance:** In spite of the media blitz that may lead students to believe that being excellent at sports or having other special talents can outweigh poor grades, this is simply not true. The best approach is to build a strong academic record that shows you selected courses that challenged you and stretched your learning.

www.petersons.com

Game Plan for Getting into College

1

2. **Standardized Tests:** What about the alphabet soup of standardized testing—the SAT I, SAT II: Subject Tests, AP, and ACT? Although strong scores on these tests are important, admissions committees view these after they review the academic performance of a student. Don't put all your eggs in one basket. Top scores on the SAT won't gain you entrance if your course selection and grade point average don't show that you've chosen an academic route that prepares you for success in college.

3. **The Essay:** This dreaded element of the college application is actually one of your greatest tools. It allows you to convey to the admissions committee those unique and special qualities that don't come through in your transcript. It is the one part of the application that is totally in your hands. Use it to make a special impression and help your application shine amid the thousands of others in the pile. You'll learn how in Chapter 5.

4. **Recommendations:** Recommendations written by counselors and teachers accompany most applications. These letters describe what the person knows about you in relation to your ability to function well in college. The writer may discuss your intelligence, motivation, critical-thinking abilities, and similar aptitudes and skills. Employer letters and letters of support from volunteer agencies may also be included to round out the picture of who you are and what you bring to a college. Choosing whom to ask to write your recommendations is important and is one of the topics in Chapter 5.

5. **Personal Interview:** Not all colleges expect to interview their candidates, but you should try to set up as many interviews as you can. The interview process may be seen as the school's way to see who you are, but you should also view it as a way to find out about the school. Who interviews you, the tone of the interview, the questions you are asked, and the answers to the questions you ask will tell you much about the philosophy of the institution and its administration. Combined with a tour of the campus, the interview can help you decide whether you want to attend a particular school. See Chapter 4 for more on the campus tour.

6. **The Hook:** What is a "hook"? Colleges strive to create a diverse community of students with different ethnic and socioeconomic backgrounds, athletic abilities, artistic flair, leadership qualities, and other characteristics. These characteristics or attributes are known as hooks. What is your special characteristic or hook? By displaying and describing your unique attributes in an effective manner, you can increase a college's interest in you. How do you do this? Your essay can broadcast your specialness, but you need to decide early in the process what to concentrate on and how to cultivate it.

As the criteria listed above illustrate, much of the college entrance process is related to self-exploration and growth. As you work on presenting yourself in the best possible way, you will be examining yourself and learning how to put your best foot forward. Getting to know yourself, appreciating your uniqueness, and knowing how to transmit it to others will determine whether your envelopes are thick or thin. In many ways, the college entrance process is a rite of passage, and it is not without growing pains. This book is an aid to your travel, a tool to help you through the passage so that you will be able to concentrate your energies and direct them in the most efficient way possible.

GETTING STARTED

As you begin the process of choosing and applying to colleges and then making your final choice, you will be bombarded with advice from a variety of well-intentioned sources. Concerned and caring parents, teachers, and relatives will pull you aside to share their thoughts about what would be your best choice for college. You'll receive tons of mail from unfamiliar colleges. Your high school guidance department will deliver reams of colored-paper packets on dozens of topics in group meetings with your class, in evening sessions with your parents, and in individual conferences with you. It has been my experience that most college-bound students suffer not from a lack of advice about their options but from the lack of an effective system to sift through and

Most college-bound students suffer from the lack of an effective system to sift through, organize, and determine what information is most useful to them.

organize the information and determine what is most useful to them. This book will help to create that organizing system.

Staying motivated, open, and curious as you explore during the next few years will keep your options open and help you make a choice that will work for you. Try not to limit your exploration in the beginning. Some students close off their options too soon because they feel that private colleges are too expensive, college course work is too difficult at competitive schools, they won't fit in at certain colleges, or they're really needed at home so they can't go away to school. I suggest that you visualize the options like a funnel—large at the top and narrow at the bottom. In the beginning, it is important to consider all your options. If you narrow your focus too soon, you may miss some great opportunities simply because you refused to look at them from the start. Stay open to new ideas.

Remember, no one person can give you the "right" answer to where you should go to college. Ultimately, you are the one who has to make the decision. In the beginning stages, however, creating a network of support around you is important. Get to know your guidance counselor, establish contacts with interviewers and alumni at the schools you're interested in exploring, confide in your friends and share experiences with them, and get to know your parents again—they should be an integral part of your support team. They can be your best supporters since they are genuinely interested in your happiness and anxious to see you succeed in college (and, in many cases, are helping you pay for it).

Having said this, I would like to add one more piece of advice. Take control of this process early and own the decision at the end of it. The earlier you feel that you are directing your exploration, the more likely your final decision will work for you. College really offers you the best route to your future. Now, how are we going to create your road map to success?

COLLEGES: ALL SIZES, SHAPES, AND FLAVORS

The first thing you will need to do is decide what type of institution of higher learning you might want to attend. There are more than 3,500 colleges and universities in the United States alone, and each of these institutions is as individual as the people applying to it. Although listening to the voices around you can make it sound as though there are only a few "elite" schools worth attending, this is simply not true. The right match for you is out there. You just have to put some time and effort into locating it, recognizing that your dream school may not be one of the big-name schools.

About half of U.S. postsecondary institutions are four-year schools that can generally be classified as either universities or liberal arts colleges. These schools grant bachelor's degrees and can be public, meaning state-sponsored, or private, meaning governed by a board of directors. Although most are coed, a few schools limit their student bodies to a single gender. Some schools have a religious affiliation, while others traditionally have a student body of a particular race. There are also five military academies supported by government funding. Some schools have a focused curriculum, such as fine arts, business, performing arts, or engineering. Of course, there are the "Ivies," those schools whose names have become familiar to us and whose stringent admissions policies—and costs—are legendary (Brown, Columbia, Cornell, Dartmouth, Harvard, Princeton, the University of Pennsylvania, and Yale).

If a four-year school seems like too much too soon, there is the two-year junior or community college option, in which students earn the first two years of a four-year college degree (called an associate's degree) either in full-time or part-time study. This option works well for people who want to remain close to home, for whom cost is an issue, or who want to hone their study skills to prepare themselves for an eventual move into a four-year school. One benefit of junior and community colleges is that they offer degrees that allow graduates to take state-sponsored certification tests (for example, in registered nursing) and then work in their chosen fields while continuing on for a

> Some schools offer courses over the Internet. If time or cost are concerns, you might check to see if online courses are available in your area of interest.

> **There are many different routes to earning a college degree, and as long as you stay focused and motivated, there is one that will work for you.**

bachelor's degree at night and on weekends. There is no set plan to achieve a college education, and no one way is better than another. There are many different routes to earning a degree, and as long as you stay focused and motivated, there is one that will work for you.

As you begin to explore your options, there are several key elements you should keep in mind: size of the school, distance from home, cost, characteristics of the student body, entrance standards, and majors offered. These are all crucial factors to consider in identifying the type of institution that is likely to fit you best.

WHERE WILL I BE MOST COMFORTABLE?

Schools come in all shapes and sizes, from tiny rural colleges of 400 students to massive state university systems serving 100,000 students or more. What if neither of these types of institutions strikes a chord with you? There are many schools that offer a compromise between the high-rise dorm cities of large universities and the proverbial leafy campuses of small liberal arts colleges. These institutions fit somewhere in the middle and often offer the best of both worlds.

Sizes and Types

If you are coming from a small high school, a liberal arts college with 3,500 students may seem large to you. If you are presently attending a high school with 3,000 students, selecting a college of a similar size may not feel like a new enough experience. Some students coming from very large, impersonal high schools are looking for a place where they will stand out from the beginning and will be offered a more personal approach. If you haven't got a clue about what size might feel right to you, try visiting a couple of nearby colleges of varying sizes. You do not have to be seriously interested in them; just feel what impact the number of students on campus has on you.

Large Universities

Frequently located in or near major cities, large universities offer a wide range of educational, athletic, and social experiences (for small universities, see page 9). Large universities are usually composed of several smaller colleges devoted to broad subject areas. Depending on your interest in a major field or area of study, you would apply to a specific college within the university. Although selection criteria for the university may be published, each college has the flexibility to set its own standards for admission. For example, a student applying to a university's College of Arts and Sciences might need a minimum GPA of 3.2 and a minimum SAT I score of 1200. Another student applying to the College of Engineering could find that a minimum GPA of 3.8 and SAT I score of 1280 are the standards. The colleges within a university system also set their own course requirements for earning a degree in their area.

Universities may be public or private. Both types of institutions offer a full scope of undergraduate majors and award master's and doctoral degrees as well. Private universities may be secular or affiliated with a religion. A few of the larger private universities, such as Yale and Princeton, are well known for their high entrance standards, the excellence of their education, and the success rates of their graduates. Universities place a great deal of emphasis on research, whether it be historical, literary, or scientific, and they compete aggressively for grants from the federal government to fund their projects. Large public universities, such as the State University of New York (SUNY) system and the University of North Carolina at Chapel Hill, also support excellent educational programs, compete for and win research funding, and have successful graduates. Public universities, however, often offer substantially lower tuition rates to in-state students while their fees to out-of-state residents are competitive with private institutions.

Outside the classroom, particularly at some large state universities, sports will likely play a major role on campus. Athletics are big business and can dominate the calendar of events and set the tone year-round at some schools. Alumni travel from far and wide to attend their alma mater's games, especially football, and the campus—and frequently the entire town—grinds to a halt when there is a home game. Athletes are heroes and dominate campus social life.

What are some of the other features of life on a university campus? Every kind of club imaginable, from literary to chorus to bioengineering, can be found on most college campuses. You will be

> Take a look at the size of the classrooms in the larger universities and envision yourself in that atmosphere. Would it offer a learning environment that would benefit you?

able to play the intramural version of almost every sport in which the university fields interscholastic teams or to join fraternities and sororities and groups dedicated to social action. You can become a member of the band, the orchestra, or perhaps a chamber music group or work on the newspaper, the literary magazine, or the Web site. Depending on the size of the campus, the list can go on and on. Does the variety of choices seem bewildering? Although you might want to try out a new interest or two, chances are you will pursue what you have always been interested in and make like-minded friends along the way.

Liberal Arts Colleges

If you have considered large universities and come to the conclusion that all that action could be a distraction, then a small liberal arts college might be right for you. Often tucked away on "picture-perfect" campuses, liberal arts colleges generally have student bodies under 5,000. The mission of most liberal arts schools is learning for the sake of learning. This focus places a strong emphasis on creating lifelong learners who will be able to apply their education to any number of careers and stands in stark contrast to the more profession-based curricula of some larger universities and specialized schools.

Because of their small size, liberal arts colleges cannot offer the breadth of courses that the large universities do. As a result, liberal arts colleges try to create a niche for themselves. For instance, a college may place its emphasis on its humanities departments, whose professors are all well-known published authors and international presenters in their areas of expertise. Or a college may highlight its science departments by providing state-of-the-art facilities where undergraduates conduct research side by side with top-notch professors and copublish their findings in the most prestigious scientific journals in the country. The personal approach is very important at liberal arts colleges. Whether it is advisement in course selection, athletic programs tailored to students' every interest, or dinner with the department head at her home, liberal arts colleges emphasize that they get to know their students well.

If they are so perfect, why doesn't everyone choose a liberal arts college? Well, the small size limits options. Fewer people may mean

> Check out the activities listed on the Student Center bulletin board. Does the student body look diverse enough for you? Is there enough happening to keep you busy and interested? Do the students have input into decision making? Do they create the social climate of the school?

less diversity. The fact that many of these colleges encourage a study-abroad option (a student elects to spend a semester or a year studying in another country) reduces the number of students on campus even further. Some liberal arts colleges have a certain look: granola, jock, feminist, artsy. All these words have been used to describe various liberal arts campuses. Will you fit in with the culture? Will the small size mean that you go through your social options quickly?

Honors Colleges

An honors college can best be described as a school within a school. In high demand because they offer what is considered close to an Ivy League education at a state school price, these colleges exist on many large public university campuses. An honors college has its own stringent admissions policies, handpicked faculty members, and attractive scholarship packages. The honors college may offer admission to a small percentage of the university's incoming freshman class, or it may require a separate application directly to the college. The major attraction of these programs is that they offer students the benefits of a large university, with all its facilities, diversity, and opportunity, while still allowing students to enjoy the rigorous academics and intimate social environment of a smaller school. Does this concept of a school within a school appeal to you? Or is the backdrop of the university too overwhelming?

Small Universities

Similar in prestige to honors colleges are some of the smaller universities, such as Washington University in St. Louis and Wesleyan in Connecticut. Highly regarded, these institutions generally have enrollments of about 4,000 students and balance the major options of large universities with a smaller campus community. Note the word *major*. Small universities offer choices but not to the same extent as large universities. On the other hand, by limiting admissions and enrollment, small universities manage to cultivate some of the characteristics of a liberal arts college. Like a liberal arts college, a small university may emphasize a particular program and go out of its way to draw strong candidates in a specific area, such as premed, to its campus.

How small is small? A small university may still be too large—or too small—for you. Will you find enough diversity in the student population, courses, and activities to interest you? Or are there too many choices?

Specialized Schools

Another alternative to the liberal arts college or to the large university is the technical or otherwise specialized schools. Their goal is to offer a specialized and saturated experience in a particular field of study. Such an institution might limit its course offerings to the performing or fine arts, engineering, or business. Schools like the California Institute of Technology concentrate on attracting the finest math and science students in the country. At other schools, like Bentley College in Massachusetts, students literally eat, sleep, and breathe business. These institutions are purists at heart and are strong believers in the necessity of focused, specialized study to produce excellence. If you are looking for a well-rounded college experience, these schools are probably not the place for you. But if you are certain that you want to immerse yourself in math or music or business, you will fit right in.

Religious Schools

Because they receive federal funding, public universities may not support any particular religion. But if religious orientation is important to you, there are many institutions that have varying degrees of religious affiliation. A number of private universities and liberal arts colleges were founded in support of a particular religion. Some have become secular institutions over time (for example, Harvard), while others remain dedicated to a particular theology and require that their students take a set number of religion courses to graduate.

Single-Gender Schools

For those who want to pursue their education without the distraction of the opposite sex, there are single-gender colleges. Although they may offer coeducational evening classes for undergraduate degrees for adults and coeducational graduate programs, the traditional under-graduate day college remains either all-female or all-male. Women's colleges especially pride themselves on turning out leaders. If you want to concentrate on your studies and hone your leadership skills, a single-gender school might be an option.

Location and Distance from Home

Besides size and type of institution, location and distance from home are two other important decisions you will have to make. If you have always lived in the suburbs, choosing an urban campus can be an adventure. But after a week of urban noise, dirt, and rude people, will you long for a grassy campus and open space? On the other hand, if you are used to the suburbs and mall life and choose a college in a rural area, will you run screaming into the Student Center some night looking for noise, lights, and people? Whether you realize it or not, the location—urban, rural, or suburban—can directly affect how easy or how difficult adjusting to college life is for you.

Don't forget to factor in distance from home. Everyone going off to college wants to think he or she won't be homesick, but sometimes it's nice to get a home-cooked meal or to do the laundry in a place that does not require quarters. Even your kid sister may seem like less of a nuisance after a couple of months away.

Here are some questions you might ask yourself as you go through the selection process: What part of the country do I want to be in? How far away from home do I want to be? What is the cost of returning home? Do I need to be close to a city? How close? How large of a city? Would city life distract me? Maybe I would concentrate better in a setting that is more rural or more suburban. Here are three scenarios to consider:

Urban

Your 11 a.m. English 101 class is right next to a Greek luncheonette, and the aromas wafting in make your stomach groan as the professor drones on. Back in your dorm, the wailing sirens of emergency vehicles on the street make sleeping an adventure most nights. Some city-based schools have central grass-covered campuses, while other schools sprawl all over town. But if you are the kind of person who needs to be at the center of the hubbub, near theaters, libraries, museums, restaurants, and people, an urban campus may be right for you.

Rural

You wake up in a quiet dorm room in an ivy-covered building steeped in 100 years of tradition. Looking out the window, you see rolling green foothills and the occasional cow. After class, you and your classmates take long walks in the college arboretum, sipping coffee and discussing your latest philosophy lecture. This setting might seem idyllic. But when it's Saturday night, you're 200 miles from civilization, and the one movie theater in town is playing the same film for the fourth week in a row, will the idyll wear thin? What seems like a picture-postcard setting on the college tour may lose its attraction after the first year, or it may be just the environment in which you thrive.

Suburban

A suburban college setting provides proximity to a city with all its attractions but also distance from the hubbub on a daily basis. You will find quiet, grass, trees, a small town nearby, and a slower pace. Two issues to consider are how far from the city you are and how you will get back and forth when you do want to venture in. If riding the subway is not your idea of a great experience but a commuter train would be all right, that can help you choose the college, city, and distance.

Other Factors to Consider

What else should you consider? A major factor is cost. What can you and your family afford? How much financial aid can you realistically expect? Are your grades good enough to win you a scholarship? How much of a scholarship? Chapter 6 will help you answer these questions.

Of course, whether you meet the academic requirements is another factor that will determine where you apply and where you ultimately matriculate. In Chapter 3, we will discuss how you can realistically evaluate your options. But remember, you have to evaluate the school, too. Does it offer you the field of concentration and the courses, especially at the upper level, that you are interested in pursuing? If you are not sure what you may want to do, which schools give you the best opportunities to test the waters before selecting a major? That's all part of picking a college.

Another factor to consider is the student body. Depending on where a school is located, its size, and its educational mission, you may find a very diverse group of students or a more or less homogenous one. Large urban schools tend to be more diverse, but smaller schools outside large cities have made great efforts in recent years to diversify their student populations. Religious schools obviously have fairly homogeneous groups in terms of values but may be diverse in the socioeconomic backgrounds of their students. The same is true of single-gender schools. When you visit a campus, look around and see if you would feel comfortable. Check activity boards and the student newspaper. Are there groups you could join that would provide support and help?

Making the Decision

As varied as each graduating class of high school seniors from all over the country is, the institutions of higher learning that accept them show just as much diversity. From traditional to avant-garde, liberal to conservative, and political to scientific, colleges and universities expand and adapt to meet the needs of their students. Schools shape themselves to the influences of a society that puts its trust in these centers of learning to provide the leaders of the future.

College is not just about book learning. It is an environmental experience that will shape you for the future. You will form the basis for the way you think about things in the years to come, and you will make contacts that will last you a lifetime. College is about establishing your independence, knowing your own desires, and having a place to test them. It's all there, but it's up to you to find the college or university that meets your needs. Trust your guidance, but listen to your instincts. Look closely at a variety of schools, get "the feel" for them, and then decide which type is right for you. After you have decided, something will settle inside you. You will know the size and location that seem most comfortable and the academic focus that holds the most appeal to you.

Trust your guidance, but listen to your instincts.

COLLEGEEZE! WHAT ARE THEY TRYING TO SAY?

"Rolling application, admit, admit/deny." Learning the language of college can be as confusing as deciding where to go. Check the Glossary at the end of this book to help you understand what colleges are really trying to say. You will come across these words and phrases as you scan the Web, read college catalogs and brochures, and attend information sessions during college visits. You don't need to memorize the definitions; just keep this list handy as you work your way through the college entrance process.

LEARNING TO PUSH THE ENVELOPE: SETTING PERSONAL GOALS

Colleges are interested in students who are going to succeed in their educational settings. After all, a school's reputation rises and falls on the performance of the students it graduates. There are limited spots available in the college pool, and institutions are seeking students who will bring with them an abundance of possibilities. Colleges and universities are not interested in well-rounded students. They are seeking to optimize their position in the academic world by admitting students with outstanding individual talents who, when merged together, will create a gifted freshman class. How do you plan your high school program to become one of the gifted freshmen?

The following is an excerpt from a recommendation I wrote for a student of mine named Josh who was applying to Ivy League colleges. I have included it here not to scare you, for he was truly an extraordinary student, but to give you a sense of what I mean by "pushing the envelope" when it comes to academics. Throughout high school, Josh chose to challenge himself with his selection of courses. The type, variety, depth of studies, range of difficulty, and the excellence he displayed showed a great deal about his true capabilities. More importantly, Josh knew how to take advantage of a learning environment, making the most of it each step of his way.

"I only await a wall I have not scaled..."

These words typify Josh's optimistic approach to learning and highlight his willingness to grapple with complex and difficult issues in his thirst for knowledge. He is capable of complex and sophisticated thought and possesses a metaphysical and poetic nature. He works intensely and carefully, thoroughly absorbed in the topic of the moment. Josh's contagious quest for knowledge ignites his peers, provoking and eliciting thoughtful discussion and raising the educational tone of the classroom to a higher level.

He is award-winning in all areas and is consistently excellent in all of his endeavors. He is a scholar-athlete, student leader, National Merit semifinalist, National Cum Laude Association member, Bausch and Lomb Science Award winner, Science Olympiad and Mathlete (including the American Mathematics Competition Award) team member, and Latin and French language competitor. Josh's achievements range from successes in music (first baritone horn), the sciences, literature, poetry, mathematics, languages, and sports to computer programming and computer business entrepreneur.

Since ninth grade, Josh has been enrolled in the most rigorous honors and AP-level academic programs offered by this high school, and he has never received less than an A. Especially proficient in languages, Josh has been accelerated in both French and Latin and will graduate with a five-year AP-level sequence in French and a four-year AP-level sequence in Latin. His outstanding scores on the SAT I and II and his 5s on the AP exams attest to his ability to excel at the college level.

Remarkable? But there is more to Josh's story, and this is why it is instructive to other students. Josh figured out how to work around a system to accomplish his goals. High schools all over the country usually have a method or sequence for advancing from one academic level to the next. In most instances, the logic that drives the method is well thought out and proven over time to work for the majority of people who pass through high school. Sometimes, though, the system is limiting for a student. Small schools may not offer all courses every year or may offer a course only one period a day because of budget constraints or teacher availability. This happened to Josh. His solution was to accelerate, skipping a level of language, studying on his own over the summer to master the information, and working after school with his teacher to ensure his mastery. "Where there's a will there's a way," and it was often Josh who came up with the solutions. This showed that he was able to develop unique and innovative strategies that worked for him.

The other element clearly apparent in the example of Josh is the number and variety of extracurricular activities and clubs in which Josh was involved. Keep in mind that he was always consistent with his involvement, sticking with and being truly committed to every activity for the four years he attended high school. This is important in the eyes of colleges and universities that are looking for students who will add to the climate of their campus when admitted. Josh never joined anything just to make a show for the transcript; his involvement was a true reflection of his interests. With his choices, Josh told these institutions who he really was.

Colleges and universities are not interested in well-rounded students. They seek students with outstanding individual talents who, when merged together, will create a gifted freshman class.

Setting Your Personal Goals

What choices should you make? It is important to remember that when you apply, colleges will see displayed on your transcript every class you have taken and every grade you have earned in high school. Because the content of the courses in the eleventh and twelfth grades mimics the kinds of material and the demands you will experience in college, admissions counselors place more emphasis on how well you perform in these classes. Colleges and universities look for growth and students' willingness to challenge themselves throughout their high school careers.

Admissions counselors can immediately pick out students who have backed off in their course selections and taken the easier road, especially in their senior year. To admissions committees, there is no such thing as "senioritis." It makes sense that if the course load is building to more complex material, the junior and senior years should reveal the most challenging courses on your transcript. If you are telling an admissions committee in your essay how devoted you are to literature but your transcript shows that you are not enrolled in the AP

English that is offered in your senior year, a red flag goes up in the committee members' minds. (Red flags are never good things!)

To ensure that you make the most of the courses available to you, set up a four-year plan with your counselor in ninth grade. This will help you to identify class availability, course sequences, and the prerequisites for the more demanding courses. Question your counselor about the requirements for graduation and for college admissions. Reviewing this plan and revising it yearly as you begin to discover your career goals and interests will ensure that you are on track to accomplish your goals.

There are some guidelines that are considered the bare minimum for college entrance:

Subject	Years	Types
English	4	Composition, literature, British literature (if available)
Foreign Language	3	Three consecutive years of the same language
Mathematics	3	Algebra I and above through precalculus/calculus
History and Social Sciences	3	European, U.S., economics, law and government
Science	3	Lab sciences such as biology, chemistry, physics

When choosing your courses, remember to push the envelope. Look at foreign language, for example, if it is a subject you really enjoy studying. Talent in languages in a global economy and the era of the World Wide Web can be an important asset. People with a good command of two or even three foreign languages will be a sought-after commodity. So go for it, as Josh did, taking five years of one language and three or four years of a second.

Remember, your high school years and the college entrance process itself are about finding out how good you really are. Testing your boundaries during high school, in the safety of your own backyard with your support network in place, will give you the confidence to venture out as the next "gifted freshman."

By the way, Josh got into the Ivy League school of his choice.

Preparing

You are dressed in your brand new school clothes, with the fastest sneakers money can buy on your feet, a lunchbox in your hand, and a book bag in the shape of your favorite animal on your back. A nice person shows you where to hang your coat, right under the sign with your name spelled in colorful letters. As you sound out the words, repeating them to yourself, this person grasps your hand and leads you into a room. There you find fourteen other children, dressed very much as you are, sitting in a circle staring at one another other. Welcome to kindergarten.

In the perfect world, you would have a perfect plan. It would begin right there in kindergarten, and you would already be aware that kindergarten would have an important impact on your future. In today's society, nearly everyone understands that an education opens doors and allows more choices. Before you ever strapped on your backpack and headed out for your first day of school, your parents had poured a great deal of time, effort, and hope into preparing you for your future. Parents dream that their children will have a chance to attend a good college, graduate, become successful in the career of their choice, and be happy.

WHEN SHOULD I REALLY START TO THINK ABOUT COLLEGE?

When is the right time to begin to chart the journey that will set you up for a smooth college application process? Before we begin to discuss the optimum plan, I want to reiterate that although there are important milestones to check off, everyone has his or her own timetable and way of doing things. *There is no one way for everyone!*

Some school districts do not offer advanced courses in middle school, some students take longer to hit their stride than others, and some lives are filled with hardships and distractions. What factors are you dealing with? To answer that question, you need to look at yourself and where you are right now honestly and nonjudgmentally. The fact that you are reading this book means you are heading in a positive direction. There are many ways to get on track and set goals no matter where you may be along the journey in the college entrance process. If you want a college education badly enough, you'll find a way to get one!

THE FOUNDATION

Education is like a pyramid, with each block building upon the others. As far back as kindergarten, you began to establish patterns of behavior that led to success in the educational arena. You developed the self-discipline to attend school every day and to pay attention when you were there. You learned to get along with others and to express your needs and wants. You learned to write down your ideas, tried out new experiences, and remembered to carry things home and bring them back to school the next day. The skills you gained in elementary school were the foundation you built upon in middle school. Your thinking, reasoning, writing, and verbal abilities matured over the course of your education, and all these accomplishments readied you for the challenges of a high school program.

Remember middle school? Those years were critical in establishing your schedule for high school. Many schools around the country provide for acceleration in middle school, which may begin with courses in grades 5 through 8. These courses may count toward high school credit if a student maintains a passing grade. For instance, a student who took a four-year middle school course (grades 5 through 8) in a foreign language, such as French, maintained a B average, and tested well for proficiency could be granted 2 high school credits.

Let's extrapolate (a good SAT word) this example across the high school years and see what impact it will have by the time this student graduates from high school. The student could begin the third year of French in the ninth grade and complete a five-year credit sequence by junior year. This would allow the student to add additional courses to his or her schedule in another area and would certainly make a powerful impression on college admissions officers.

WHAT DO I DO NOW?

Fine, you say, but you're already in high school, and you didn't accelerate any courses. My motto is "it's never too late." But we need to look back before we can look ahead.

Remember back to eighth grade, when a group of high school counselors arrived at your middle school with course selection sheets? They explained that you would have several different teachers a day, that the school year would be divided, and that you would need to choose courses and electives. Twenty minutes later, you were looking at the selection sheet trying to figure out what the electives were and how many the counselors said you needed to check.

You made some important decisions at that juncture, hovering between middle school and high school, and those decisions are having a profound impact now on your schedule in high school. As an example, consider how your beginning math class dictated the level of math you would be able to achieve by the time you graduated. Because math is sequential, meaning the concepts follow and build on one another year after year in a logical manner, it is very difficult to make up for lost time by leapfrogging a course or doubling-up on courses. Whenever possible, you should try to persevere through three or four years of high school mathematics, terminating with precalculus or calculus.

Course Sequencing

For those of you who just groaned, let me explain why this concept is so important. Colleges and universities have what are called core requirements. You are already familiar with this concept because it is similar to high school graduation requirements that state you need, say, 4 years of English, 3 of history, 3 years of science including 2 with labs, and so on, adding up to 24 high school credits. Most colleges will require that you take about 60 credits in core courses that they establish and require for graduation regardless of your major. I promise you that at least one of these core courses will be a college-level math. In order to have a foundation in high school that will prepare you to comprehend the information presented in the college-level course, you need to take as many math courses as possible in high school. If you need help grasping the concepts, you have more support around you while you are living at home than you will have living away at college. You can get extra afterschool help from your high school teacher, attend the high school math lab, create a study group with friends, or obtain the services of a tutor, if that is economically feasible for you and your family.

Level of Courses

Another factor that you need to consider is the level of the courses you are taking in high school. Are the courses remedial, regular, honors, or Advanced Placement? Colleges and universities want to see what they perceive as a college-preparatory program. The course level you may take is based on how your performance is perceived by your teacher the previous year. Students who master the subject matter, contribute in class, and earn a B average or better will likely be recommended for an honors-level course when they advance to the next grade. Most school districts have guidelines for offering advanced courses that carefully delineate the standards of performance required, steps in the process of selection, and reasons for placement. Some schools have very rigid standards for admitting students into honors and AP-level courses. Schools want students to feel successful during their high school experience, so the tenuous balance between challenging a student and overwhelming him is carefully considered.

You and your parents should discuss your options each year before you decide on your course schedule. A word of advice: If you are recommended for an honors or AP-level course, take it! The course demands at these levels will help you gain the knowledge and skills you need to succeed in college. Remember that a B grade in an honors or AP course has a more positive impact on college admissions officers than if you received an A in a less challenging course.

How will colleges know the difference, you ask? You are probably not the first person who has graduated from your high school and applied to that college. In addition, admissions counselors receive a profile from your school that lists every honors and AP-level course offered. The admissions counselors look at your transcript, compare it against the profile, count the courses you have taken, and compare the number and levels with the number and levels available. Voila! They see

Six Study Skills That Lead to Success

1. **Set a regular study schedule.** No one at college is going to hound you to do your homework. Develop the study patterns in high school that will lead to success in college. Anyone who has ever pulled an all-nighter knows how much you remember when you are on the downside of your fifth cup of coffee and no sleep—not much! Nothing beats steady and consistent study habits.

2. **Save everything.** To make sure your history notes don't end up in your math notebook and your English papers don't get thrown at the bottom of your friend's locker, develop an organized system for storing your papers. Stay on top of your materials, and be sure to save quizzes and tests. It is amazing how questions from a test you took in March can miraculously reappear on your final exam.

3. **Listen.** Teachers give away what will be on the test by repeating themselves. If you pay attention to what the teacher is saying, you will probably notice what is being emphasized. If what the teacher says in class repeats itself in your notes and in review sessions, chances are that material will be on the test. So really listen.

4. **Take notes.** If the teacher has taken the time to prepare a lecture, then what he or she says is important enough for you to write down. Develop a system for reviewing your notes. After each class, rewrite them, review them, or reread them. Try highlighting the important points or making notes in the margins to jar your memory.

5. **Use textbooks wisely.** What can you do with a textbook besides lose it? Use it to back up or clarify information that you don't understand from your class notes. Reading every word may be more effort than it is worth, so look at the book intelligently. What is in boxes or highlighted areas? What content is emphasized? What do the questions ask about in the review sections?

6. **Form a study group.** Establish a group that will stay on task and ask one another the questions you think the teacher will ask. Compare notes to see if you have all the important facts. And discuss your thoughts. Talking ideas out can help when you have to respond to an essay question.

that you did not take everything that you could have. Why not? they ask themselves. There's another red flag, and remember, you don't want red flags.

"It's Never Too Late"

How about you? Maybe you were not tuned into the nuances of course selection or the logic of a math sequence back in the eighth grade.

Maybe you are just now hitting your stride and realizing college might be for you. Or maybe you have moved around so much that with each new school you have lost ground or been ineligible for an honors-level course because you do not have the prerequisites from previous schools. What options are open to you? As the following recommendation I wrote for another of my students demonstrates, it's never too late to turn things around.

Delightful, gregarious, innately intelligent, gentle, and easygoing, Mark has not only made a most remarkably rapid adjustment, but he has been able to leave an imprint in the two years since his arrival. Mark went from being a mediocre student in a large, impersonal high school, to a B or better student in a more demanding but smaller and more personal one. The changes required of him were not insignificant: developing good study habits, adopting a positive and enthusiastic attitude about learning, and disciplining his mind.

Mark's work habits have been surprisingly good this semester, and although we have found that he has gaps in his education (understandably), he has been willing to seek help and try to fill them in. Mark found that a particular teacher was teaching a creative writing class and asked if he could sit in. Mark began to do the assignments, read his work aloud, critique other students' work, and, even though it "didn't count," became a contributing member of the class.

When Mark first came, he had little interest in extracurricular activities, but over time has become an enthusiastic participant in such activities as photography club and band. Mark also plays his guitar in informal pick-up groups. He has been employed over the last two summers in part-time jobs. His most recent New York City office job included 10- to 12-hour workdays.

About two years following his parents' divorce, Mark split his living arrangements between two households, spending four days at each house. The expectations in the two households were very different.

*Perhaps his expertise at balance and negotiation of contradictions
emerged from his adaptation to his two environments. Mark's prior
poor scholastic performance may be related to a strategy of
navigating between a structured and a lax household. There is a
correlation between Mark's move to a single household that provides
him with a stable and supportive environment and the improvement
in his schoolwork.*

Mark's story is unusual, but if he can make up for educational deficien-
cies, so can anyone who wants a college education badly enough.
Remember: Take at least a four-year sequence in each of the "big five"
subject areas and challenge yourself with the toughest courses you can
get into. But what else should you do?

BEYOND THE CLASSROOM

As you plan your high school career, there are two areas in addition to
course work that you need to consider—academic competitions and
extracurricular activities. The level and types of competitions and
activities may not only impress college admissions committees, but
they also add immeasurably to your high school experience. They help
you test out your interests, stretch your abilities, validate "how good
you are," and teach you valuable knowledge and skills.

Academic Competitions and Special Programs

During your high school and even your college career, many of you will
have opportunities to exhibit your academic strengths and artistic
abilities through competitions, contests, or involvement in special
programs. These opportunities exist in a broad range of areas. There
are foreign language competitions that allow you to earn certificates
attesting to your advanced language abilities. National math and
science competitions are known for admitting only the finest science
students for consideration. There are writing competitions that result
in publication or even production of the winners' work. Competitions
in multimedia art, the performing arts, and technical and scientific
areas allow you to demonstrate your unique abilities and receive

feedback from renowned figures. Winning these competitions may open doors to scholarships and once-in-a-lifetime experiences. Summer invitational programs held at university campuses all over the world offer exciting opportunities for academic growth and international travel.

Over the years, I have heard many excuses from students who are reluctant to enter into this level of competition or who hesitate to investigate an opportunity. Some reasons are legitimate, and personal limitations should always be respected. However, considering how much you can gain from these experiences, if you approach them with the right attitude, it is important to think twice before passing them up.

What is the right attitude? The most common and positive response I have heard from students who have participated in competitions is that they allow participants to measure themselves against other people who have displayed excellence in their same field of interest. Think about it. You may be the proverbial big fish in a small pond at your school, very familiar with the other students and with no one new to bounce your ideas off. What better chance will you have to exercise your mind and test your ideas against some of the other brightest students in the country? This is true whether you attend a program or event to compete or to assess your skills through competitive national tests and written compositions. Students who have traveled to compete for debates, engaged in science and math competitions, or had their writing published come out of the experience more self-assured. Whether they won recognition or not, these students entered into the experience openly and gained from trying.

This kind of excellence and initiative go a long way to convince a college that it wants you to attend its institution. Recognition from nationally defined and accepted organizations is easily understood and interpreted by admissions officers. If your academic competitions involve travel or living away from home for a time, the comfort level and emotional maturity that this demonstrates reassure a college that you can handle being away from your family. This is a big concern for colleges because many of the freshmen who do not return for the second semester or who drop out during their sophomore year do so because they are unable to make the adjustment to living away from home.

Extracurricular Activities

As you already know, there is life beyond the classroom, and not all learning is accomplished at school. You also probably know that extracurricular activities are viewed positively by college admissions people. But what should you get involved in? Whatever it is, don't get involved just to earn "brownie points" for college. Participate in activities based on a genuine interest in what you join, and stick with what you join. The activities in which you participate and your commitment to them are reflections of who you are.

There is also a great deal more to be gained from extracurricular activities than just impressing admissions officers. Extracurricular responsibilities help you learn new things about yourself. You can develop leadership abilities or learn how to work in a team. You might enhance your communication skills, learn more about the "world of work," or just get satisfaction from doing something kind for someone else. Involvement in extracurricular activities may lead to internships or jobs in the future, but it will certainly build your resume and give you an outlet for your abilities. Extracurricular activities can teach you how to prioritize, divide your time, and balance your schedule. Most of all, if you choose extracurricular activities wisely, they will give you satisfaction, improve the quality of your life, and help define you—not just for college admissions but for life.

Now let me explain how this kind of involvement impacts the college admissions process. Colleges send mixed messages about involvement in extracurricular activities. On the one hand, they tell students to choose activities that appeal to them. On the other hand, they want student leaders, state champion athletes, and nationally recognized scholars.

What are you supposed to do? Before you choose any activity, think carefully. You know it will be hard to stick to something you hate doing simply for the sake of your transcript. If you do not like competition and shudder at the thought of getting up at 5 a.m., then joining the swim team for that varsity letter is not for you. Don't try to tailor your involvement to match what you think colleges might be seeking. This is the time to figure out what you want to do—and then find a college that appreciates you for doing it. If you like to write, join the school newspaper or literary magazine. If you are a whiz in math, then mathletes is for you. Your school doesn't have mathletes, you say? See about organizing a math club and competing.

What is going to be different about you? Sometimes it is the way you describe your involvement that makes the difference. Take a look at the following activities and see what a difference using more unique phrasing can make. But it is more than just the way you say something. All of the categories in the left-hand column are worthwhile and offer many choices for student participation. Within each category, there is room for individualism and the possibility for beginning new projects and being the "first." Remember, extracurricular activities can be as diverse as the people who participate in them.

Activity	Standard Statement	Unique Statement
Athletics	Junior and senior varsity track, tennis, and wrestling	• Ice hockey, wind-surfer, snowboarding competitor • First student at school named to All-State Baseball Team
Community service	Volunteering at hospital, nursing home, animal shelters	• Organized meals-on-wheels program • Tutored children and adults in local literacy program
School/ community leadership	Class officer, club officer, athletic team captain, editor of school publication	• Wrote grant for local cleanup project • Led group against substance abuse
Band/ chorus	Participated in orchestra and band; member of state choir	• Member of award-winning a capella group • Started local radio program

How Colleges Look at Extracurriculars

Colleges and universities are a living microcosm of our society. They are interested in inviting students to join their freshman classes who will bring with them more that just their GPAs. The student body lives together, often forming small cities. Colleges want to attract students who will help establish vibrant, stimulating, and enthusiastic communities. Admissions counselors and college administrators are very sensitive about the "mix" of the classes they admit. They want outstanding athletes and performing arts talents, activists and the community service-minded, high school newspaper editors and class officers, writers and musicians, rugged individualists, the politically leftist and rightist, feminists and environmentalists, the culturally diverse, small business entrepreneurs, techies, and the student who has maintained a part-time job with the same employer throughout high school. In other words, colleges and universities want a wide range of interesting people who will share their interests with others.

I have said this before and I will say it again. High school is about trying out new things to see how they feel. Joining activities and playing sports that you have never tried before are part of what high school is for. How else will you know if they are for you? But as I have also said before, colleges like to see consistency when it comes to involvement. Once you have found something you like to do and that you think is a reflection of who you are, stick with it until you graduate from high school. Don't collect activities for the sake of collecting because you think a long list will win over an admissions committee. Colleges want to see that you have been involved with the same activity for three or four of your high school years and that you have achieved, whenever possible, a leadership role. Above all, a college or university wants to know that you are multifaceted and will be able to balance your education with a full and enriching life experience on its campus. In addition, seeing your involvement in and commitment to a diverse range of activities reassures a school that you will be an interesting contributor to the texture of its student body. Schools want strong, intelligent, inventive, and dynamic people—just like you!

> Many students do great things for their schools and for their communities, but they never stop to think that they should tell colleges about their activities. When I speak to these students about how impressive their involvement is, they get embarrassed. Don't. Learn to be your own best advocate.

Talking With Your Parents

The first conversation you have about college should be with your parents or guardians. This conversation should happen early and may need to be revisited as you get closer to making final plans. Make an appointment for this discussion, and pick a time convenient for everyone. Don't make it one of those "I-just-came-in-the-door-it's-late-Sunday-night-and-I-want-to-talk-about-my-future" conversations. Everyone should think about the discussion ahead of time, because this is the time for all of you to air your questions, thoughts, and fears about the entire process. The discussion with your parents or guardians should include topics such as:

Be mature, patient, and listen to one another now. An honest and sincere conversation will open communication lines and begin developing the kind of mutual support team you will need as you work through the college entrance process.

- What are their feelings about the college process and you?

- Do they have definite ideas about the maximum distance from home they would like you to be?

- Are there financial concerns and constraints?

- Has anyone established for you an educational fund or a state prepaid program that has set aside tuition for you as long as you attend a public school within that state?

- Are there college legacies, or traditions, in your family? Are your parents contributing alumni members of a college(s)? In both of these cases, your family's affiliation with a school might improve your chances of getting in.

- Do your parents' employer(s) offer scholarship grants or matching funds for scholarship money received from other sources? If one or both of your parents are employed by a university, does it have a program providing tuition-free or reduced-cost admission to employees' children? Does it have similar programs with partner institutions?

- Can everyone in the family agree that this is a personal experience for you that does not have to be discussed with others—in or out of the family? Respect for your privacy, sensitivity about your feelings, and support during a time when you are trying to make a decision that will have a tremendous impact on your future can go a long way to reducing stress for the entire family in the upcoming months. If you feel strongly that your plans are not for public consumption, be sure to let your family know early on.

- What are your parents' expectations for your academic performance in order for them to continue supporting you financially while you attend school? What other expectations do they hold for you during your college years?

- Are your parents willing to agree to and support your final decision? (Remember, it is your decision.)

These are all important points, and raising them early will do a great deal to prevent hurt feelings, misunderstandings, and a last-minute change in plans down the road. I have seen countless instances when a student went through all the right steps, researched college options, and identified the dream college only to find that the family really could not afford it. Don't let this happen to you. College can be expensive, but there are affordable alternatives and tactics to help pay for it. If everyone recognizes this from the beginning, you can plan your strategies from the start.

Besides finances, get the record straight on other issues, too. How did your parents react to your dream of going to college in Hawaii, 5,000 miles from home? Not too well? This kind of disparity can become a real sticking point for them and for you. The thought of leaving home and being on your own with no one to tell you to turn down the stereo at 11 p.m. may sound like heaven now. But try to look at it from another perspective. Moving away from home also means moving away from the familiarity and comfort of the places you have probably known for much of your life. The cost of an airline ticket from Hawaii is a serious consideration, especially come Thanksgiving when it seems as though everyone you know has headed home for the holiday. Some of your parents' concerns may be self-motivated, for this is certainly a major change in their lives, too. Keep in mind, though, that after seventeen or eighteen years of raising you, they might have a pretty good idea about what will work best for you. Do they have concerns about your ability to handle the adjustment, life choices, or course load at a college that is far away from home? Their fears may be groundless, but it will help to air them openly to ease one another's concerns.

What if your parents have their hearts set on your attending a particular school? Your dad's office is filled with coffee mugs and banners from his alma mater, and your family has held season tickets for its football games since before you were born. Your dad remembers what a grand old time he had there, and he wants you to experience it too. "What do you mean you want to look at other colleges?" he asks you incredulously. As far as he is concerned, there aren't any others. When there does not seem to be much room for discussion, how should you proceed? Carefully and with an open mind. If you just cannot tolerate the thought of attending the school your parents have their hearts set on, you need to state your case clearly and firmly. Don't let it degenerate into whining. Steer clear of criticizing the school your mom or dad loves. Instead, explain to them what you are looking for in a college, how you want to try something new and all your own, and how schools X, Y, and Z will help you do just that. Chances are, once you present your side of the story in a calm, mature way, they'll remember that this is about what is right for *you*.

With all that said, don't resist dad's alma mater just because he is pushing you to go there. Legacy is a big word with colleges, particularly the Ivy League and the more competitive schools. Do not overlook its ability to open doors. Many of these schools hold a strong commitment to their alumni and take in up to 30 percent of each year's freshman class as legacies. The bottom line might be that without the power of a legacy, your mother's or father's school might be way off the chart for you based on your test scores or your GPA.

Talking With Your Guidance Counselor

Once you have talked with your parents and understand the role your family is able and willing to play in your college selection process, you should plan a conversation with your guidance counselor. This should really be a series of conversations with the goal of allowing this person to get to know you. After all, he or she will be an advocate for you during your high school experience. Guidance counselors do more than input your schedule into the computer and meet with you to determine whether you are making the progress you need for graduation. Guidance counselors are a valuable source of college information and serve as a crucial link in your connection to the college of your choice.

As you begin your junior year, the first things you want to get from your counselors are a "College Planning Timetable" and a "College Planning Guide," also known as a "College Exploration Packet." These are devices developed by most guidance offices to help keep you on schedule in the selection process and to highlight some of the milestone dates and events along the way. These two documents point out key informational resources available at your school and list the steps that should be taken to secure your goal of entering the school of your choice in the fall after senior year. See Appendices A and B for an example of each document.

> You are not alone in this process. Many experienced and sincere people are available to help you on your way. Remember to acknowledge their time and help with thank-you notes. It makes a great impression and keeps them motivated!

Whatever has been developed as your school's packet has been put together as an aid to you. If you stuff it in your locker, leave it on a desk in a classroom, or bury it in your backpack, you have lost some valuable information that can save you time and energy. I tell my seniors that this year in their lives is "trial by fire." Once they have completed their college selection process, the four years of college will seem like child's play. All of the forms, tests, tours, and whatnot that go into choosing a college can start to seem overwhelming, especially if you try to take it on by yourself. Let your counselor assist you. We have been through it many times before!

Gathering Information From Colleges

Once you have spoken to your family and your guidance counselor, it is time to begin gathering information about the colleges themselves. In this early stage, you are fact-finding, searching for basic information about different schools and their offerings. Your best bet is to go straight to the colleges for this type of information. Whether you have a clear picture of the schools you are interested in or just have a general idea of the types of institutions that might appeal to you, now is the time to go straight to the source and start finding out what you will need to know to make decisions later on. Check the "Sample Request for Information" form in Appendix D to learn how to contact the schools.

A great starting point for this, once you have come up with a general list of schools to inquire about, is a college guide such as *Peterson's 4-Year Colleges*. You can read about the schools you want to learn more about and find the contact information for the various people with whom you need to get in touch. Also, many schools have Web sites where you can learn more about their departments, faculty, and student body. If you are an athlete, you should contact the coaches of your sport at the various colleges. E-mail or write them with your questions. Be sure to investigate scholarships and open team positions. Maybe you are interested in drama. Contact the drama department to learn about the productions they put on last year. Find out as much as you can about what interests you.

Bear in mind that there are cycles in college admissions offices. The most hectic time is winter when admissions committees are reviewing applications and making final decisions. If you are a tenth- or eleventh-grade student looking for information, spring is the best time to seek advice from colleges. A word here about information overload caused by asking too many people too many questions: Choose your sources wisely and keep track of valuable information in an organized manner. Then you will be able to refer to it later when you make your final list of colleges.

ALPHABET SOUP

It's May, the weather is starting to heat up, and so is the college pressure. You are a junior, it is the weekend before the SAT, and you have finally gotten around to studying. On your bed is a pile of paperback review books, your computer screen glows bright with the words SAT Practice, and you have just found the crumpled sample test booklet your guidance counselor gave you in January. So what if it is stained with chocolate from being stuffed in your backpack for five months? You can still make out most of the words! Sweat pours down your forehead and your heart pounds because you have heard that this test will determine whether you find the doors to college open or closed. Why didn't you look at this stuff before now? Your father has been hounding you about it for months! Suddenly the alarm clock rings, and you breathe a deep sigh of relief. Like Scrooge awakening from a long night, it's just a bad dream. It's really only January.

This is a wake-up call for all of you out there who want college in your future. Begin early to familiarize yourself with the SAT and the other tests you will be taking. Every year, millions of high school students are tested. The College Board and American College Testing, Inc., the masterminds behind the SAT and ACT exams, administer more than 7 million exams annually. These are not the first tests you have taken, and they will not be the last. You have had pop quizzes,

---

The Top 10 Ways Not to Take the Test!

- Cramming the night before the test.
- Not becoming familiar with the directions before you take the test.
- Not becoming familiar with the format of the test before you take it.
- Not knowing how the test is graded.
- Spending too much time on any one question.
- Not checking spelling, grammar, and sentence structure in essays.
- Second-guessing yourself.
- Forgetting to take a deep breath to keep from—
- Losing It!
- Writing a one-paragraph essay.

---

classroom tests, unit exams, midterms, and finals. Chances are, you have also taken some form of standardized test administered by your state or school district. Tests are part of your life and will be throughout your educational experience.

A word about taking tests seems in order. All these tests have already given you an idea of the type of test taker you are. Some students take tests in stride: "Okay, another test. Let me write it down on my calendar next to the other three that day." Other students become anxious and worry that they will not do well, thus making it difficult to do well. News flash—not everyone who gets A's on tests is brilliant. A large part of how well one does is based on attitude, but most of what makes the difference is strategy. Many learning centers will tell you, "It's not just how smart you are; it's how smart you take the test."

The PSAT, SAT I, and ACT

The major standardized tests students take in high school are the PSAT, SAT I, and ACT. Colleges across the country use them to get a sense of a student's readiness to enter their ivy-covered halls. These tests, or "boards" as they are sometimes called, have become notorious because of how important they can be. There is a mystique that surrounds them. People talk about the "magic number" that will get you into the school of your dreams.

Beware! There is a lot of misinformation out there. First and foremost, these are not intelligence tests; they are reasoning tests, designed to evaluate the way you think. These tests assess the basic knowledge and skills you have gained through your classes in school, and they also gauge the knowledge you have gained through outside experiences. The material on these tests is not curriculum-based, but the tests do emphasize those academic experiences that educational institutions feel are good indicators of your probable success in college. (See pages 40–53 for specific information on each standardized test, including the SAT II Subject Tests and AP tests.) There are many fees and deadlines associated with testing. Application fees, late fees, score report fees, rushed score fees, withholding fees, removal fees, duplicate fees—the list goes on and on. This is another instance when it is crucial that you spend time with your counselor to learn how the testing system works. To keep the fees from mounting up, watch your deadlines and plan when and where you want your scores sent. Your guidance department will have the criteria and necessary forms.

> If your high school places test scores on the back of transcripts, check a copy for accuracy. Find out if the schools you are applying to will accept these posted scores as official. If they do, it will save you some money on sending official test reports.

Test Scores and College Admissions

How does standardized testing fit into the college entrance equation? As I mentioned earlier in this chapter, your grades and the level of the courses you take will carry the most weight in the college selection process. If you have not selected a college-preparatory course load and kept up with your grades, good SAT scores are not going to save you at the last minute. On the contrary, putting all your eggs in one basket is a bad idea. Standardized test scores should be a reflection of your cumulative knowledge and academic performance in school. When colleges and universities see scores that are way out of proportion to a student's GPA and the quality of the courses taken, a red flag goes up. (Remember: No red flags!) Admissions committees start asking questions like: What was this student doing throughout high school? Was this student choosing not to challenge herself? Are these scores valid or a fluke? Will this student know how to use the opportunities we have available and be successful here?

There needs to be a correlation between what admissions counselors see on your transcript and the scores you earn on standardized tests. These scores will be viewed with the other parts of your application, probably second or third in order of priority. Recently, standardized testing has received less emphasis, especially among highly competitive liberal arts colleges.

Even if you are planning to apply to a college that does not require SAT I or ACT scores, it would be prudent for you to have them in your records for the future. You might enter a college that does not require these scores, only to decide halfway through sophomore year that you want to transfer to another school. At that point, are you going to want to sit through a standardized test? Having the test scores will allow you more freedom of movement.

A Few More Words About the SAT

Because the SAT I figures so large in your college selection process, I want to say a few words specifically about the SAT process. First, know your test-taking calendar in advance. Registration for the test is about six weeks before the test date. Don't register late, because late fees can add up. Before you start to fill out the test application, find out where you want to take the test and the codes for the test center and for your school. You can sign up on line for the SAT I (and all the College Board tests) at www.collegeboard.org or by phone. Check your application booklet for the correct toll-free telephone number. You will need a credit card to use either method.

Watch your test-taking timetable carefully and revamp it if things change for you. For example, if you take your first SAT I and get a 1520, you probably don't need to take the test again. The same is true of your SAT II Subject Tests scores and schedule. Your counselor will get a copy of your test results. Discuss with him or her how your test results compare with the range of scores for college entry for previous students from your high school. Your school has a track record of entry statistics with colleges, and your guidance department can make this information available to you. Knowing where you stand in the range can help you decide whether you need to take the test again.

If you feel you have bombed a test, it is possible to cancel your scores within 24 hours by calling the College Board. Be careful about doing this, however. I can't tell you how many times I have had students in my office upset because they were sure they had blown a test only to find out the next day that they had gotten a 90. In your anxiety, you may not be reading your performance correctly.

Remember that SAT score reports are cumulative, meaning that the College Board establishes a history for you of all the SAT I tests you take. When you request a score report be sent to colleges, the score for every test you have taken will appear on it. Think carefully about the implications.

Recently, standarized testing has received less emphasis, especially among highly competitive liberal arts colleges.

- When you take the test, be prepared. This score will be seen by your colleges of choice.
- Do not sit for an official test for practice. There are other ways to practice.
- With multiple test scores, colleges will give you the benefit of the doubt in most cases. If you take two SAT I tests and the first test has a higher math score than the second one, colleges will split the scores from both tests, giving you the higher math and verbal SAT scores in your application records with them. However, if you take the SAT three or four times and have not prepared evenly for each testing situation, your scores will reflect this. This will present a roller-coaster effect to the colleges. Because they cannot get a clear picture of what your "real" performance is, they will find the average of all of your scores. This will work against you.

A Few More Words About the ACT

Because more than 1 million students now take the ACT each year, I want to provide some additional specific information about that test, too. Like those of you taking the SAT I, know the dates for the administration of the ACT. Registration is five to six weeks before the test date. There is a late fee and a standby fee, so don't procrastinate about registering. You can sign up on line at www.act.org or by phone. You will need either a Visa® or MasterCard® for both online and phone registration.

It is possible to cancel your score by calling ACT by noon on the Thursday following the test. Check the registration booklet for the correct number. But before you cancel, think twice. Did you really do that badly or do you just think you did? There is really nothing to lose by having the test scored. You control the release of your test scores. ACT will send only those score results you tell it to. If you have taken the test more than once, ACT, unlike the SAT, does not automatically report past test results to your list of schools. In other words, if your score is higher for the ACT you took in April of your junior year than for the test you took in October of your senior year, you can have just the April test score sent. If you like all your scores, you can also instruct ACT to send all your scores, past and current.

Is there any advantage to taking the ACT more than once? The ACT folks will tell you that if you had trouble understanding the directions, felt ill during the test, really think that the test scores do not reflect your abilities, or have taken additional course work or a review course, you should think about taking the test again. ACT publishes statistics that show that of students who take the test as juniors and retook it as seniors, 55 percent increased their composite score, 22 percent had no change in the composite score, and 23 percent decreased their composite score. The average ACT score in a recent year was 21 out of a possible 36.

A Word About Coaching

Coaching is a huge issue in standardized testing today, and the pros and cons are still being debated. In many affluent communities, the perceived need for coaching is part of the culture. In other areas, test-prep courses are seen as an unnecessary extra. The short answer is that there are some students who take professional review courses and see a dramatic increase in their scores, while there are others who take the courses and see little change. Two things tend to hold true. A set schedule of self-review and a longer review program seem to produce the greatest gains.

What should you do? First, think about how you can best spend your time and energy. How will you balance reviewing for the test with your academics and present schedule of extracurricular activities? Are you the kind of person who needs to sit in a regularly scheduled class to fully benefit from learning? Is enrolling in a course where you need to commit six to eight hours for eight weeks a good use of your time? These courses review the entire test. What if you only need to spend time on strategies or maybe only the verbal section? The extra time commitment may interfere with your ability to keep up your grades. *Remember: Grades are your number one priority!*

Perhaps study guides, online sites, and CD-ROM programs where you can dictate your own time and sections for review will better meet your needs. There are also private tutors available at $60 to $75 an hour to meet with you around your schedule. They will hone in on your specific needs. Every student is different, and there are many options available for test prep. Talk to your counselor about a test study schedule, the best study guides, and whether enrolling in a review course might work for you.

PSAT/NMSQT

Why Take the Test?

The Preliminary Scholastic Assessment Test/National Merit Scholarship Qualifying Test (PSAT/NMSQT) is an early practice test for the SAT I. More than 2 million students take the PSAT each year. The types of questions that appear on this test are identical to the ones you will see on the SAT I. The format of the two tests is also the same. The test is given in October, and you will have your results by December, which allows you plenty of time to set up a study schedule for taking the SAT I in May or June. In 1998, for those who had taken the PSAT/NMSQT, the mean SAT I score was 129 points higher than those who had not taken the earlier test.

The PSAT reports what are called *silent scores.* Only you and your guidance counselor see your scores. They are not reported to colleges. This allows you to "practice without penalty" in a timed setting similar to the testing circumstances you will find for the SAT I. The test results, which are provided in a detailed, easy-to-read form, are an excellent tool to help you determine those areas where you need extra help and study.

Depending on your score on the PSAT, you may be able to enter the national scholarship competition run by the National Merit Scholarship Corporation. Finally, the PSAT provides schools with the information that you are interested in attending college, which means that colleges and universities will put you on their mailing lists.

TEST FORMAT

There are five sections, with a total testing time of two hours and ten minutes, and there are two breaks. The Verbal Reasoning portion of the test contains multiple-choice questions that involve sentence completions, analogies, and critical reading. The Math Problem-Solving section contains multiple-choice questions and student-produced response questions that cover arithmetic, algebra, and geometry. The multiple-choice questions in the Writing Skills section ask you to improve sentences, identify sentence errors, and improve paragraphs. There is no essay.

Area Tested	Number of Sections	Number of Questions	Time Allotted
Verbal	2	52	25 minutes/section
Math	2	40	25 minutes/section
Writing Skills	1	39	30 minutes

What to Bring

- PSAT entry card or your name on the guidance list for entry
- Several **sharpened** #2 pencils
- Identification, preferably with a picture, such as a driver's license or school ID. You could also bring a copy of your transcript or a note from the guidance department on school letterhead attesting to your identity. *ID will be checked at the test!*
- Calculator. Any four-function scientific or graphing calculator will do. Do not bring a calculator with the memory the size of a computer or one with a noisy typewriter-like keyboard. Do not bring a laptop, an electronic writing pad, or a pocket organizer. If

you bring a calculator with a display screen so big that it can be seen by others, the test supervisor may decide not to seat you. Also, your calculator cannot speak to you, have paper tape, or require an electrical outlet.

- Leave the following at home: loud watches, CD players, tape recorders, cell phones, pagers, and school supplies. You will not need scratch paper, notes, books, dictionaries, compasses, protractors, rulers, highlighters, or colored pens or pencils. You might want to bring some fruit juice, tea, or water and a healthy snack for the breaks.

Timing

Traditionally, students have taken the PSAT in October of their junior year so that they can use the score for the National Merit Scholarship Qualifying Test. The NMSQT compares the scores of juniors across the country. Above a certain cutoff, students are able to enter the competition for National Merit scholarships.

In recent years, it has become more common for students to take the PSAT in October of their sophomore year. About 33 percent of test takers choose this route. Taking the PSAT this early allows students and counselors more time to plan schedules to meet students' academic needs and better prepare them for their career choices. However, taking the test in October of your sophomore year does not enter you into the National Merit Scholarship competition.

Strategies

- Know the format and timing of the test. The best way to do this is to practice, practice, and then practice some more. Purchase review books and take the practice tests in them and in the Student Bulletin (see page 56). Make a schedule and set aside a regular time to practice. Isolate yourself and try to simulate a testing environment when you practice.
- Know the directions for each section and type of question. The directions are the same on the PSAT as they are on the SAT I. It will save you time during the real test if you do not have to read the directions.

Quick Facts:
The fee for the PSAT is $9 to $12, depending on the administration fees your school sets. The PSAT lasts 2 hours and ten minutes plus one break and has 131 questions. The PSAT is scored on a scale of 20 to 80 for each subject. Adding a zero to the end of a PSAT score shows you the equivalent SAT I score.

- Learn how to make educated guesses. All but ten questions on the PSAT are multiple-choice. You need to be able to eliminate at least one answer as wrong, however, before making your best guess.
- Build a vocabulary bank. Read, read, and read some more. No amount of drills, flash cards, or memorizing words out of context is going to help you own these words. Pick up a Sunday newspaper and read the editorial section every week. Read it with a dictionary next to you. Then do the crossword. These two activities alone will grow your vocabulary about 800 words a year.

SAT I REASONING TEST

Why Take the Test?

The majority of colleges and universities across the country require either the SAT or ACT. In scheduling the date to take the test, be aware that scoring the test can take six to eight weeks. The SAT must be completed and scored and a test report from the College Board sent to the colleges of your choice prior to their application deadlines. Sending test reports to schools not on your original SAT application will cost you $6.50 each.

Most juniors take the test at least once. Fifty percent take it twice, which allows you at least one chance to show improvement.

What to Bring

See the PSAT, page 41, for dos and don'ts.

Timing

The SAT I and SAT II Subject Tests are given on the same test dates—the first Saturday of each month from October through June. You can use a test date for either the SAT I or SAT II, but not for both.

Most juniors take the test in May or June. This works well because, for the most part, they have completed their course of study for eleventh grade. They can use this knowledge for the test, and it also gives them time to review their PSAT results. The tests are scheduled before final exams, which leaves time to study for both. Take either a May or June test; do not sign up for both. The results of the May test will not be returned to you before you sit for the June exam. You need time to see how you scored on the first test so that you can establish a study schedule to address weak areas and raise your next scores.

TEST FORMAT

There are seven sections, with a total testing time of three hours. The seven sections can appear in any order and vary that of the student sitting next to you. Three types of verbal questions are used: analogies (19 questions), sentence completion (19), and critical reading (40). These questions measure knowledge of word meanings, test the ability to see the relationship in word pairs, assess understanding of how parts of sentences fit together correctly, and measure the ability to read and think carefully about a single reading passage or a pair of related passages. The math portions include 35 multiple-choice questions that test knowledge of basic math concepts, algebra, and geometry; 15 multiple-choice questions that test the concepts of equalities, inequalities, and estimation; and a grid-in portion of 10 questions.

Area Tested	Number of Sections	Number of Questions	Time Allotted
Verbal	3	78	two 30-minute sections, one 15-minute section
Math	3	60	two 30-minute sections, one 15-minute section
Experimental (math or verbal)	1	1	one 30-minute section

No one timetable, however, fits all needs. For example, some juniors might be applying to colleges that require three SAT II Subject Tests. Or they might be taking AP courses as juniors and want to take the AP exams in May. If you are facing decisions like these, you might consider other timing options for the SAT I. Talk to your counselor. You may be ready to take your SAT I earlier in order to leave time for the AP or SAT II exams.

Strategies

- Know that the detailed personal profile questions in the center of the SAT I application form are optional. The statement of intent is the only area that must be copied and signed in the center. However, the information that you provide on the personal profile will enable colleges to identify your interests. If there is a match, you will receive material from them to help you with your college selection process.

Know that test questions of the same type are grouped together and range from less to more difficult, except for the critical reading section. Start with the easy questions and do not linger over any one question too long.

Know that the test is scored differently. Each correct answer is worth one point, and a portion of a point is deducted for incorrect answers except in the grid-in portion of the math test. No points are lost for omitting a question.

Understand that you are not expected to know everything on the test. If you answer half the questions correctly and omit the rest, you can still get an average score.

Grid in carefully and use the correct answer sheets for the right sections. Erase completely and follow the directions for gridding the student-response questions.

Remember that the directions and question types are the same as the PSAT. You are already familiar with them. Each minute you save reading the directions is a minute more you can spend taking the test.

> **Quick Facts:** The fee for the SAT I is $23.50 for students applying on time (with a late fee of $15 and an additional $15 fee if you go standby). The SAT I is three hours long and consists of 138 questions. The maximum score for each section is 800. The total maximum combined score is 1600.

ACT

Why Take the Test?

There was a time when the ACT was offered as an alternative to the SAT, but more and more it is being used by students in certain parts of the country as their primary—and sometimes only—college entry test. In twenty-five states, more than 50 percent of the students take the ACT as compared to nineteen states for the SAT. This is the result of greater acceptance on the part of admissions offices of the ACT as a predictor of success at their colleges and universities. All the Ivy League institutions accept the ACT.

Test Format

There are nineteen sections and 215 questions, with a total testing time of 2 hours and 55 minutes. With breaks, you will be there for 3½ hours. The multiple-choice–only test covers reasoning in English, math, reading, and science. Spelling and vocabulary are not tested. The English section tests usage, mechanics, and rhetorical skills. The math portion consists of questions on algebra, geometry, and trigonometry. The reading section has passages from the social and natural sciences, prose fiction, and the humanities. Data representation, research summaries, and conflicting viewpoints are the subjects of the science questions.

Area Tested	Number of Sections	Number of Questions	Time Allotted
English	5	75	45 minutes
Math	5	60	60 minutes
Reading	4	40	35 minutes
Science	5	40	35 minutes

The ACT, unlike the SAT I, is curriculum-based. It tries to measure what students have learned in their classes, and, by measuring this knowledge base, it tries to predict their success in college. Since knowledge is cumulative, the test is targeted to juniors in high school. Because the ACT is comprised of subject tests, those colleges that require SAT II Subject Tests will often take the scores on the ACT exams in lieu of the SAT II tests. For students for whom English is their second language, the fact that the ACT is comprehension-based will sometimes offer them a better chance at achieving a high score.

For students who are planning to enter a junior college, the ACT is an excellent test to take. It may be used by the colleges for placement into appropriate course levels. If you are interested in a junior college, be sure and check if it is used. The ACT has added an interest inventory section in which students respond to a series of questions about their interests. Along with their test scores, students receive a graphic and descriptive section about particular careers to explore.

What to Bring

See the PSAT, page 41, for dos and don'ts.

Timing

A September testing date is available in some states. This date is not used by the SAT program, so it allows students to focus their attention on this test only. Otherwise, with the exception of no February test date in New York, the test is given five times a year from September until May. Some students will take the test in June of their junior year.

If you are using the test for placement purposes or taking the test to have "one in the bank," meaning you are applying to colleges that do not require either the ACT or SAT or are not planning to enter college right after graduation, register for the test in December of your senior year. If you later change your mind about going on to college and find that a standardized test is required, you will have one.

Strategies

- Look at both the SAT I and ACT and the requirements of your colleges to determine which one you should choose.
- Review before you take the ACT. Because the test is content-oriented recent, participation in the subject and/or thorough review of materials will increase your score.
- Know the test format. This test is very different from the SAT, so you will need to become familiar with the ACT's approach and format. For one thing, the ACT does not penalize you for guessing.
- Know how the ACT reports scores. ACT scores are reported differently than SAT scores. If you take the test more than once, you may choose which score you want sent to schools.

- This is different from the SAT, where each time you take the test your score is placed on your score report in a cumulative fashion. ACT will only release those scores that you specifically request. I think you can figure out the strategy here. There is an intricate balance between trying to put your "best foot forward" and integrity. Many colleges are beginning to request that all scores be reported to them or they may ask a question on their application addressing this point. If you are asked directly, respond honestly. Approaching this process with integrity is always the best way to enter a college that will be a good match for you.

> **Quick Facts:** The fee for the ACT is $22 in most states and $25 in all others (with a $15 late fee and an additional $30 if you go standby). Each of the four areas of the test is scored from 1 to 36. A composite score is derived from these four and sent to colleges.

SAT II SUBJECT TESTS

Why Take the Test?

The SAT II Subject Tests (formerly known as the Achievement Tests) measure a range of knowledge in a broad variety of subject areas and the ability to apply that knowledge. The subject tests are used for two purposes. Some colleges and universities use them to determine whether a student meets their standards for admission, and scores may also be used to determine placement in college courses for entering freshmen.

Test Format

The SAT II Subject Tests are subject-specific, presently administered in 22 different subject areas. Each test is one hour long, and most are multiple choice. For the reading and listening test, the listening portion is administered first, followed by writing. The following subjects are offered for testing under the SAT II program: Writing, Literature, American History, World History, Math Level IC, Math Level IIC, Biology E/M (Ecological/Molecular), Chemistry, Physics, French (reading only), German (reading only), Modern Hebrew (reading only), Italian (reading only), Latin (reading only), Spanish (reading only), Chinese (reading and listening), French (reading and listening), German (reading and listening), Japanese (reading and listening), Korean (reading and listening), Spanish (reading and listening), English Language Proficiency (reading and listening).

What to Bring

See the PSAT, page 41, for dos and don'ts.

Timing

Given throughout the school year starting in October, SAT II Subject Tests coincide with SAT I dates, but not all SAT II tests are given on each date. You may register for as many as three SAT II tests on each date.

If the SAT II Subject Tests are to be used for placement purposes, students may elect to take the SAT II Subject Tests in the spring of their senior year, as long as they can stay motivated to do well. If using the tests for entry purposes, students have several options. Juniors might take the SAT II: Writing Test and one other SAT II test in April. They might then repeat the Writing Test in June and take one or two additional SAT II tests. In October and November of senior year, students might take additional SAT II tests or repeat earlier ones to raise their scores. Most students take the Writing Test more than once because there is a component of this exam that is graded subjectively. It is an important test and the one most requested by colleges.

Scoring may require anywhere from six to eight weeks. Consider this when you are calculating your admission deadlines. Your testing should be completed a minimum of nine weeks prior to your deadline. It is sometimes possible to submit a note to the admissions committee to say that you are having scores of a recent testing rushed to the school and to request that it holds its consideration of your application until this last piece arrives.

Strategies

- Schedule a test as close to completing a course in that subject as possible. If you are presently earning a strong A in a regular course or a B in an honors-level course, consider taking a test in that subject.

- Review the content for each test. There is a definite advantage in setting up a study schedule and refreshing your knowledge of the information.

- Limit to two the number of tests that you take on any test date; it will probably achieve the best outcome for you. Although you may sign up to take as many as three tests in one sitting, you will need to devote ample time for study in each subject area to ensure that you have covered the materials on the test.

- Know that you may change your mind on the day of the test about the number of tests you want to take. If you signed up for three tests and decide at the test center to take only two, you need only to notify the test administrator at the site. There will be no refund.

- Know that you can also change your mind on the day of the test about which tests you are going to take. Test centers are given extra exams for this reason.

Quick Facts: The fee for each test is $13. The scoring for the SAT II is similar to the SAT I. The maximum score is 800 per test.

- Know that for the listening tests students may be required to bring their own cassette players that comply with testing requirements or cassette players may be supplied by the test center. Check the requirements ahead of time.
- Make sure you know which test schools require as you make your final college list.
- Know that Score Choice is available for SAT II Subject Tests only. Score Choice allows you to sign up on your application or make the request at the test center to have your scores withheld until you release them. Colleges that require SAT II scores for admission usually request three tests. By implementing Score Choice you can take several different tests or repeat the same test more than once without having any scores reported to the colleges. After receiving your test results, you choose which test(s) on which date(s) you want released to your colleges. You can use several methods to send reports: go on line, call, use Score Sender, or fill in the school codes on the Additional Report Request Form that is mailed back to you with your entry slip. You will be charged a fee for each college if you use Score Choice unless you are sending these scores as part of other SAT test reports.
- Use SAT II Subject Tests to highlight your strengths. Supplement your application with the SAT II Subject Tests in those subjects in which you are not taking an AP-level course. Whenever possible, test in your junior year because it is that transcript and test scores that will be reviewed by colleges for entry.

AP TESTS

Why Take the Test?

Advanced Placement courses are an excellent opportunity to build your academic skills and knowledge base for success in college. The rigorous curriculum in each subject area mimics the academic demands of college-level work. AP scores are easily interpreted by colleges and universities because they provide comparability among differing curricula in the same subject area across the nation.

Test Format

Twenty subject areas are tested through thirty-three exams. Most tests are approximately 3 hours in length, but they range from 2 hours to a little more than 3 hours. The tests contain large sections of multiple-choice questions, but there are also sections called free response, which are student-generated. The exceptions are the Studio Art exam, which consists of a portfolio assessment; the modern language exams, which include the recording of student responses on audiotape; and the music theory exam, which includes a sight-singing task. This explains the long delay between test administration and receipt of grades. The following subjects are offered for testing under the AP Program: Art (History, Studio), Biology, Calculus, Chemistry, Computer Science, Economics (Macro, Micro), English (Language and Composition, Literature and Composition), Environmental Science, French (Language, Literature), German Language, Government and Politics (U.S., Comparative), History (U.S., European), Human Geography (in 2001), International English Language, Latin (Literature, Vergil), Music Theory, Physics (Electricity and Magnetism, Mechanics), Psychology (Introductory), Spanish (Literature, Language), Statistics.

AP scores are applied by colleges in different ways. Some schools will grant credit for AP courses if you receive a 4 or 5 on your exam. Often, these scores are used to determine placement in college-level courses for incoming freshmen. The test reports are not meant to influence college admissions decisions, only placement.

The extra credit achieved by applying your AP credits to your required core college courses can make a lighter freshman course load. You could also use the credits to get into advanced-level courses in those subjects and, therefore, concentrate your studies in the areas you find exciting and interesting. Explore the possibility of obtaining a double major or use the credits to accelerate your college graduation. However you apply your AP credits, they are a good investment to hold on to for security.

What to Bring

See the PSAT, page 41, for dos and don'ts.

Timing

AP tests are administered beginning in early May, in morning and afternoon sessions. Students usually take the tests in their junior and senior years as they complete their courses in the subject matter. You may run into a situation where you might be testing in two subjects in the same time period. Notify your test administrator, and arrangements will be made for you to take both tests on the same test date. You sign up for your AP test in the guidance office, and more than likely the tests will be given in your own school.

Strategies

- Check with your high school administration for the school's policies describing the criteria for placement in AP courses and then talk with your teachers and your counselor for their recommendations. Students are usually enrolled in their junior or senior year as a culminating experience to their high school course work. For instance, a student who has completed four years of Spanish would be enrolled in AP Spanish as a fifth year. There are always exceptions. Students who display a solid foundation and understanding of their subject matter along with good study habits can have excellent success in AP courses in the lower grades.

- Before signing up for an AP course, consider the balance between your academics and the other commitments in your life. AP courses place a heavy demand on students to complete homework assignments and prepare adequately for testing. Consider carefully the number of AP-level courses you can realistically fit into your schedule. The thought and dialogue that need to go into the decision should involve your support team, teachers, guidance counselor, and the school administration.

- Before signing up for an AP course, find out if the AP test is mandated by your high school as part of the final course grade.

- Check your colleges' requirements carefully to see if they will accept AP scores posted on your transcript as official. Unless your high school has a policy that automatically reports AP scores on transcripts (and most high schools do), you can choose which colleges will receive your AP scores. You are responsible for generating a score report from the College Board to the college(s) of your choice. But if the colleges accept the scores on the transcript, you can save some money.

Quick Facts:
The fee for each AP test is $76 (with a $40 late charge). AP scores range from 0 to 5. Colleges that participate in the program will usually grant college credit for scores of 4 or 5. Some grant credit for a score of 3 in a foreign language.

- Carefully check colleges' policies regarding the number of AP credits they will award as you make your final list of colleges. Each AP score of 4 or 5 will usually be granted 3 credits by most colleges. However, some colleges are writing policies that limit the maximum number of credits granted for AP-level courses to 12.
- Don't enroll in an AP course to look good on your transcript and then blow off the test. Colleges like to see that you have challenged yourself by enrolling in AP courses, and they usually weight them in their system. They would rather see a C in an AP-level course than an A in a less challenging one.

TOOLS AND RESOURCES

Here are some print materials and Web sites that will help you learn more about each of the standardized tests you may need or want to take as part of your college entrance process.

Print

The *PSAT/NMSQT Student Bulletin*, *Taking the SAT I*, *Taking the SAT II*, *AP Course Description* booklet for each subject area, and *Preparing for the ACT Assessment* booklet are available from your guidance counselor. These booklets include a complete description of the tests, testing tips, and sample questions with explanations. You will learn more information about their scholarship programs and get mini-practice tests for free.

Web Sites

- **www.act.org** offers a full set of sample test questions and answers, strategies, and descriptions of each section on the ACT. You can also register on line for your test dates. **ACTive Prep**^{TM} is the new site for test-prep and college information offered through ACT. Practice on the ACT tests and then use **InterACTive**

University to guide you through a personalized test-preparation program using real ACT questions.

- **www.petersons.com** and **CollegeQuest**^{SM} at **www.collegequest. com** are rich sources of free information easily downloaded from the Web. You will find everything from discovering your interests to help and practice with standardized tests, user-friendly assistance with your college search, tips on essay writing, and scholarship searches.

- **www.collegeboard.org** offers hints, strategies and practice on line. Download the "Plan for College" and take the PSAT/ NMSQT flyer right off the net. Check out **EssayPrep**^{TM} to practice for the SAT II: Writing Test. Find out about **One-on-One with the SAT**®, a software program that helps you review for the test. A sample for downloading is available free. You can also register on line for all your test dates.

Which College Is for You?

So far in this book, you have learned more about academics and how to keep on track, investigated how to explore who you are through extracurricular activities, and gotten a better sense, I hope, of how to prepare for success in college. You have read about the importance of practicing for the PSAT and SAT and reviewed a great many facts about the types of colleges and universities that exist. Now it's time to talk about how to search for the right place for you.

ESTABLISHING A FOUNDATION FOR THE SEARCH

Imagine that it is a year from now and you are attending the college of your choice. You are on your way back to the dorm from a late-night talk with a friend. You keep replaying your friend's words: "I hate this place. I can't imagine why I decided to come here in the first place. I never really looked into it. Everyone told me it was a good place for me. Lots of kids from my high school applied here. They all knew the name. The first time I saw the place was when I pulled my suitcase out of the car to move in. What was I thinking?"

It's sad that your friend feels like this, but you don't feel the same way. You like it here. Sure, there are times when you miss your friends from high school, your room at home, and a home-cooked meal, but the decision you made about choosing this college feels more right to you every day. What made the difference? you ask yourself.

Maybe it was the way I approached looking at colleges in the first place and the questions I asked myself. I remember my sophomore-year English teacher saying, "The reason I am so intent on the amount of reading I ask you do for this class is to prepare you for the expectations that college will place on you. You're all heading in that direction, and we have a responsibility to give you the kind of foundation you'll need to succeed." I began to think: Am I headed in that direction?

It was obvious to my English teacher that I was going to college, it seemed obvious to most of the kids in the class with me, and, of course, it was obvious to my parents. But was that what I wanted to do with my life? Was it important to me to go to college? What was my goal in life? I spent some time during tenth grade figuring this one out. I looked at alternatives, went to guidance with a couple of friends, and did an interest inventory and a career search.

The decision was coming down to me—no one else could make it for me. I asked myself some hard questions. What did I want to achieve with a college diploma? Would I go to college to broaden my knowledge or to get specific training? Was I smart enough to handle college? How hard did I want to work? What did I do well? What were my strengths? And my weaknesses? How did I feel about learning? Were there things I really liked learning about? What mattered to me? What were my values? What kind of place would reflect my values? Could I be self-directed enough to accomplish four years of college? Would I be ready to go to college right after high school? Was I thinking about college for the financial rewards or to gain a profession? The self-evaluation wasn't easy. I envied those kids around me who seemed to know from birth what they wanted to do.

Sometime during that self-exploration, I decided that yes, college really was my choice, too. Once I had made the decision, it felt right.

When it came time to decide where I wanted to go to college, I went back inside myself again and asked more hard questions. What am I like? What's my personality? What do I like and what do I dislike? What are my views on things? Am I conservative or liberal, traditional or eccentric? Am I a rugged individualist? Do I accept differences in others? Do I only feel comfortable around certain types of people? Do they need to be of the same race as me? Am I easy to get along with? Am I quiet or outspoken? What things do I feel very strongly about? Is it important to me that the college of my choice has a recognized name? Is my religion important to me? What do I do for fun, and what makes me happy? Am I a sports fanatic or a techie? Am I city person or a suburbanite? How do I feel about going to school in the country?

I took my time—that's part of a good self-appraisal. After all, how was I going to know what to look for in a college if I didn't know who I was and what I wanted?

Some of the things I discovered about myself were new; some were hard to accept. I wanted to think of myself as open to everything. To be honest, I discovered I really wasn't, but I could live with that for now. College might introduce ideas that could challenge my way of thinking, make me question my values and expand my views. Now, that's a good reason for going.

Once I had answered my questions, I began my search. I looked into majors, size, location, distance from home, whether I wanted to go to a university or a college. This, too, took time and more and more reading. I found that colleges have personalities. By visiting campuses and talking with people at the colleges, I could apply my newly acquired self-knowledge to find those colleges that matched my personality. When it came time to choose, I had all the information—about myself and the colleges—that I needed. Looking back at it now, I put some hard work into finding the college I chose, but it was worth it.

Take your time. That's part of a good self-appraisal. After all, how will you know what to look for in a college if you don't know who you are or what you want?

If you want the above to be you a year or two from now, content with your choice of college because you knew who you were and could match your personality with that of a particular college, you need to sit down and have this conversation with yourself now. It is time to objectify your subjective feelings about yourself and the schools out there. By putting your ideas down on paper, you will be able to realistically match your own needs and traits with college and university profiles. After all, do you want to go to the school that you *think* feels right or that you *know* feels right?

The next few pages recreate a tool that I have found helpful in working with students who are trying to develop a sense of who they are, what they want from a college, and how to correlate that to the colleges that are available. Working out your ideas on paper will help you concretize (a good SAT word) your thoughts. Doing the work now can save second thoughts later.

THE MATCHING GAME

Read each question and respond by circling Y (Yes), N (No), or C (Combination). Complete all the questions and return to the top. Highlight each action that coordinates with your answer, and then read it. Where you chose C, read both actions. Look at your sheet. Is there a pattern? Do the questions seem to lead to a certain type of college or university? Certain size? Certain location? Read the suggestions at the end of "The Matching Game" for more ideas.

Question	Yes/No/ Combination	Action
1. Is it important for me to go to college?	Y/N/C	Y: Continue with your search. N: Investigate other options, meet with military recruiters, check into vocational schools, and see your counselor.
2. Do I have a goal in life?	Y/N/C	Y: State it._____. N: Don't worry, many students start college without knowing what they want to do. Look into colleges that specialize in the arts and sciences.
3. Do I know what I want to achieve with a college diploma?	Y/N/C	Y: List specifically what those goals are._____ N: Think about what college can offer you.
4. Do I want to broaden my knowledge?	Y/N/C	Y: Consider a liberal arts college. N: You might need to consider other options or educational opportunities.
5. Do I want specific training?	Y/N/C	Y: Investigate technical colleges or professional training programs in universities. N: You don't know what you want to study. Only 20 percent of seniors who apply to college are sure.

Question	Yes/No/ Combination	Action
6. Am I smart enough to handle college?	Y/N/C	Y: Think about how far you want to push yourself in college. Look at competitive colleges or an Ivy League institution. N: Look more closely at your transcript. Ask your counselor to help you evaluate it.
7. Am I willing to work hard?	Y/N/C	Y: When you are visiting colleges, ask students about handling the work load. N: Check the work load carefully. If no one is on campus on a sunny day, it may not be the school for you.
8. Am I self-directed enough to finish a four-year college program?	Y/N/C	Y: Consider only four-year colleges and universities. N: Maybe a two-year junior or community college is a better way to begin your college experience. Also consider a tech/vocational school.
9. Do I know what I do well?	Y/N/C	Y: Consider how your abilites relate to majors. Identify some._____ N: Spend a little more time asking yourself questions about your interests. Speak to your counselor and do an interest inventory.
10. Do I like to learn?	Y/N/C	Y: College is for you. A liberal arts college's philosophy is about learning for the sake of learning. N: Would a different experience make learning more exciting? Look into training programs. Are you seriously willing to give college a try? Try a flexible curriculum such a co-op or internship program.
11. Do I like to spend time learning any one subject more than others?	Y/N/C	Y: Check to see what some majors are in that area. _____ N: Look at your high school courses. Do you like any of them better than others? Which ones? _____
12. Do I know what matters to me and what my values are?	Y/N/C	Y: Look for the schools that talk about the values on their campus. Do they have an honor code for students? Do the values confirm or conflict with your values? N: Values are less important to you, so places that really expound their values may seem confining to you.

Question	Yes/No/ Combination	Action
13. Do I need to be in affluent surroundings?	Y/N/C	Y: Look at the schools that deliver that package. Check the small, private liberal arts colleges. N: How strong is your reaction against this setting? If it is strong, check larger, more diverse settings, like an urban school.
14. Am I going to college for the financial gains?	Y/N/C	Y: What majors are going to give you the payback you want? Look at business colleges and professional programs, like premed. N: If a big financial payback does not interest you, look at social service majors, like counseling, teaching, and social work.
15. Am I focused?	Y/N/C	Y: Search out the programs that will offer you the best options. N: Avoid those schools whose programs are not strong in your focused area.
16. Am I conservative in my views and behavior?	Y/N/C	Y: The political policies of schools are important. Look into them carefully. You might look at the schools in the Midwest or the South. N: If you're a liberal, look closely at the political climate. Check the schools in the Northeast and the West Coast.
17. Do I need to be around people who are similar to me?	Y/N/C	Y: If you are African American, check the historically black colleges. If socioeconomic level or a certain look is important to you, study the student populations carefully during campus visits. If it is religious orientation you are interested in, look into religiously sponsored colleges and universities. N: Look at large, midsize, and small universities in urban settings.
18. Are the name and prestige of the school important to me?	Y/N/C	Y: Look into the Ivies and the competitive schools to see if you are eligible and what they offer you. Broaden your search to include other colleges and compare their offerings for your specific needs and interests. N: Don't exclude the well-known institutions if they fit in every other way.

Question	Yes/No/ Combination	Action
19. Do I like sports?	Y/N/C	Y: Large universities with Division I teams will give you all the sports you need—as a competitor or a fan. If you do not want to compete at that level, check schools in other divisions. Look at the liberal arts colleges for athletes. N: Look into smaller universities and liberal arts colleges with good teams.
20. Am I a techie?	Y/N/C	Y: Check for computer engineering courses at technical universities and large universities near research centers and major computer business areas. Ask about hardwiring, e-mail, and computer packages before you enroll. N: It still helps to know what computer services are available where you enroll.
21. Do I need to live in or be near a city?	Y/N/C	Y: How close to a city do you need to be? In the city or an hour away? Do you still want a campus feel? Consider these questions as you visit campuses. N: Do you need space, natural beauty, and peaceful surroundings to think? Look into small liberal arts schools in rural and suburban settings. Explore universities in the Midwest and South.
22. Will I need counseling for support?	Y/N/C	Y: Investigate the quality of student services and the mechanism for accessing them. Smaller schools often pride themselves on their services. Look at liberal arts colleges. Universities connected to medical centers often provide extensive services. N: It is still good to know what is offered.
23. Do I need an environment in which questioning is important?	Y/N/C	Y: Liberal arts colleges, honors colleges, and smaller universities place an emphasis on academic inquiry. N: You like to hear others discuss issues, gather as much information and opinions as you can, and think it over by yourself. Try the university setting.

Question	Yes/No/ Combination	Action
24. Am I an active person who needs stimulation and lots of people?	Y/N/C	Y: Consider universities, large and small. N: Look at quieter schools in rural areas.
25. Do I move to the beat of my own drummer?	Y/N/C	Y: Search out schools where you feel free to be you. Look into artsy liberal arts colleges (For an idea of what I mean, check Hampshire College in Massachusetts), larger university centers near cities, and performing and fine arts schools. Y: On your college tours, check the mainstream politics of the campus and look at the students. Do you feel you would fit?

Suggestions

Here are some ideas for you to consider based on the way you answered the questions.

1. If you answered *no* to numbers 1, 3, and 4, why not investigate apprenticeships, vocational/technical schools, military enlistment options, and certification or two-year college programs?

2. If you answered *yes* to numbers 5, 14, and 20, technical or professional colleges and universities with hands-on training may give you the direction you are looking for.

3. If you answered *yes* to numbers 10, 12, 13, and 23, you are leaning toward a liberal arts setting.

4. If you answered *yes* to numbers 6, 7, and 8, examine the competitive and Ivy League colleges.

5. If you answered *no* to numbers 12, 13, 17, or 23 and *yes* to 19, 20, and 21, larger universities may offer you the best options.

Once you have completed your self-evaluation, made a decision whether college is for you, have some ideas about your personality and likes and dislikes, and can relate them to the different personalities of colleges, it is time to gather information. It needs to be quality information from the right sources. The quality of information you put into the search now will determine whether your list of colleges will represent a good or a bad match.

WHAT ARE THE BEST RESOURCES?

Students today are different than they were twenty years ago. Put a mouse in their hands, a computer monitor and a keyboard in front of them, and off they go. This is an advantage because many of the resources and connections that students need for college and career planning are available only through this electronic connection. You can research jobs, explore career options, and search colleges to a degree your parents and even older brothers and sisters could not imagine. Take a virtual visit to a university on line, e-mail questions to department professors, or communicate with students about issues that are specific to your interests. Then apply on line, saving weeks of data processing time to input your information. Visit Web sites like CollegeQuest.com and use software programs like the Guidance Informational Services. Complete your FAFSA form (the federal government's method of determining financial need for college grants and loans), sign up for the SAT (and study for it), and order information directly from colleges.

All this is brought to you through the magic of the Web. But beware. Something else can come with the Web—information overload—unless you learn a valuable new skill: information management. As you begin to look at what is available in the college exploration process, you will find no scarcity of resources. However, finding a logical way to gather the information from expert and reliable sources is the difficult part. Before you sit down in front of the computer to make magic happen with your flying fingers, start with some of the people around you who have years of experience in the process. Before tackling the online connection, you need a coach to help you plan your strategy.

People Connections

There are several human sources of information you should consult, including your teachers, your parents, the colleges you are interested in, and adults in careers you think you might be interested in pursuing. The people to start with are in your high school's guidance department.

Game Plan for Getting into College

12 Ways to Choose the Wrong College

1. Your boyfriend or girlfriend is going there.
2. Your friends are going there.
3. The tuition is low.
4. Because of its party-hearty reputation.
5. The college brochure or university guidebook showed all these fun students sitting under trees.
6. A computer college matching program said this was your best choice.
7. You visited just that campus and didn't want to look elsewhere.
8. It's located in your city or state and you didn't consider other locations, even though you could have.
9. It's the one college you and your parents have heard of.
10. You know you'll be accepted there.
11. Because of its prestige.
12. It has the academic program you're looking for, so the campus atmosphere doesn't really matter.

Your Guidance Department

Guidance counselors pride themselves on getting to know their students, advocating for them, and developing and refining information-gathering strategies to help them. Guidance counselors are dogged about staying on top of new college and career placement information. They have developed a perspective on your school that is not available through any other source. They know about the rigors of your individual school's curriculum and how that relates to acceptance statistics at universities. They have a databank on the placement of seniors from your high school in colleges all over the country. These data include statistics—GPA/HPA, test scores, level of extracurricular activities or special attributes, and genders—from individual colleges and universities about placement decisions for students from your high school across several years. Using this databank, you will be able to compare your school's placement record to the information you gather as you research each college.

Guidance counselors are terrific problem solvers. So if you are running up against a situation where your needs are outside the usual mold, a counselor can help you develop a strategy and connect with resources to break the mold. For example, you want to do advanced work, say, in a language not offered at your high school or take an AP science course not offered in a particular year. Your guidance counselor will canvas the local colleges, join with you in getting permission from the department chairs and administration to take the course for credit, and help you with the registration process.

One of the greatest helps that guidance counselors provide is information. They stock the guidance suite or career center with the most reliable resources they can find. Today, guidance counselors must be information managers, able to locate information quickly, reduce vast amounts of material to its most meaningful level, and deliver it in the most effective manner to large numbers of students. Shelves of college bulletins, catalogs, and applications must be organized and accessible. The next time you are in the guidance office, take a look at the offerings in the bookcases and on the shelves.

The more your guidance counselor sees you and learns about you, the easier it is for him to help you. Stop by to talk about your progress or just to say "hi." Ask if you can help in the guidance office. All this information management does not happen without hours of the counselors' time, usually after school. If you have skills they can use, here's a great place to volunteer.

> **The more your guidance counselor sees you and learns about you, the easier it is for him to help you. Stop by to talk about your progress or just to say "hi."**

Your Teachers

Use your teachers as resources, too. That is what they are there for. Many of them have had twenty to thirty years of experience in their field. They have taught thousands of students and watched them go off to college and careers. Teachers often stay in contact with graduates and know about their experiences in college. Ask your teachers how prepared graduates typically feel they were for college-level work. It can be reassuring to find out how well educated you are as a result of your hard work and your high school preparation.

Ask your teachers, too, about their views on the colleges you are exploring. What is their opinion based on? What do they feel about the match between you and your choice schools? Do they think you are prepared enough to succeed in that environment?

Colleges and Universities

Don't forget to go to college fairs. Usually held in large cities in the evening, they are free and sponsored by your local guidance counselors' association and the National Association of College Admissions Counselors (NACAC). The admissions counselors of hundreds of colleges, vocational/technical schools, and universities attend college fairs each year. Whether your questions are as general as what the overall cost of education is at a particular institution or as specific as how many biology majors had works published last year, the admissions office works to assist you in locating the people who can answer your questions.

It would be helpful for you to meet with your guidance counselor to develop a list of questions to ask before you attend a fair, but even if you cannot make an appointment, do not miss this opportunity. Bring a shopping bag for all the information you will get. When you arrive, get a copy of the directory of schools in attendance and locate the schools you are most interested in. Go to them first. Ask your questions, take notes, pick up brochures, and file it all when you get home.

Admissions officers also visit schools. Don't forget to attend these meetings during your junior and senior years. Generally, college admissions counselors come to a school to get a general sense of the high school and the caliber and personality of the student body. Although it is difficult to make an individual impression at these group sessions, the college counselors do take names on cards for later contact, and you will occasionally see them making notes on the cards when they are struck by an astute questioner. It is helpful to attend these sessions because consistent contact between a student and a college is tracked by colleges and universities. An admissions decision may come down to examining the size of your admissions folder and the number of interactions you have had with the school over time. Consistency pays off, so when you are really interested in a college, let the admissions committee know.

Your Parents

In Chapter 2, I pointed out that a continuous dialogue with your parents or guardians needs to be maintained throughout the college selection process. They have opinions and valuable advice. Listen to them carefully. Try to take in all their information and see if it applies to you. Does it fit with who you are and what you want? What works and what doesn't work for you? Is some of what they say dated? How long ago were their experiences and how relevant are they today? Take in the information, thank them for their concern, compare what they have said with the information you are gathering, and discard what doesn't fit.

> What major are you interested in? Talk to family and friends who work in related fields or arrange an internship and speak to your employers about their educational experiences.

The Paper Connections

As I said before, there is no scarcity of resources about colleges and universities. Many of these resources still come in that old-fashioned medium known as print or hard copy.

Using Colleges and Universities as Resources

College and university brochures and catalogs are a good place to start your paper search, and they are free. You get them by requesting them either by mail or e-mail (see the "Sample Request for Information" in Appendix D). After reading a few, you will discover that some offer more objective information than others. You will also start to learn what information colleges think is essential to present. That's important. If a college's brochure does not present the same information as most of the other college brochures, you have to ask yourself why. What might this say about the college's academic offerings, athletic or extracurricular programs, or campus life? What does the campus look like? How is the campus environment presented in the brochure? The brochures should present clues to what schools feel are their important majors, what their mission is, and which departments they are spending their budgets on. Take the time to do these informational resources justice. They have a great deal to say to the careful reader.

Reading this information before you meet with college admissions officers visiting your school or before you take a campus tour will help make you an educated consumer. It will also reduce the possibility that you will ask questions that are already answered in their material.

Using College Guides

College guides are those thick volumes you see in bookstores and the guidance office. They enable you to make comparisons between and among colleges and universities using the same criteria each time. What information do they contain and when should you use them? Let's examine *Peterson's 4-Year Colleges* to answer those two questions. Updated annually, the guide contains researched information on every accredited four-year college in the United States—more than 1,000. Guides like *Peterson's* contain categories such as:

- Location and Size:
  These attributes are displayed in an alphabetical listing by state of every college in that state. This is a good resource if you have learned that you are eligible for scholarships because you reside in a particular state and you want to know what possible college choices you have. Colleges are also listed alphabetically so that if you have the name of a college and want additional information about it, you can locate it easily.
- Freshman Application Contact:
  This section lists the mailing address for the admissions office of each college.
- Cost/Financial Aid/Tuition and Payment Options:
  This section describes the yearly expense for tuition and fees associated with a particular college and the average financial aid package offered during the previous year. Payment options available through the financial aid office are also described.
- Entrance Requirements:
  This is a great resource to look at early—ninth grade is a good time. This area lists the GPA, SAT/ACT scores, and class rank

that applicants need in order to be admitted to a particular school. Some guides also list the course sequences that should be completed in high school to be competitive for that college.

- Complete Majors Directory:

  Is what you are interested in studying available at this school? This section will give a sense of the majors and the focus of majors at any given college. The most popular majors are also listed.

- Entrance Difficulty

  How difficult is this college to get into? What do you need to be competitive? Colleges are listed as:

  - Most Difficult:

    More than 75 percent of the current freshmen were in the top 10 percent of their high school class and scored above 1310 on the SAT I or above 29 on the ACT. Thirty percent or fewer of the applicants to this class were accepted.

  - Very Difficult:

    More than 50 percent of the current freshmen were in the top 10 percent of their high school class and scored above 1230 on the SAT I or above 26 on the ACT. About 60 percent or fewer of the applicants were accepted.

  - Moderately Difficult:

    More than 75 percent of the current freshmen were in the top half of their high school class and scored above 1010 on the SAT I or above 18 on the ACT. About 85 percent or fewer of the applicants were accepted.

  - Minimally Difficult:

    Most current freshmen were not in the top half of their high school class and scored somewhat below 1010 on the SAT I or below 18 on the Act. Up to 95 percent of the applicants were accepted.

  - Noncompetitive:

    Virtually all applicants were accepted regardless of high school rank or test scores. Many public institutions are required to admit all state residents.

> Develop a system for storing the college materials you receive in an easily retrievable manner. Try file folders or oversized envelopes, labeled with the names of each college. Make sure each packet includes an application form.

- Athletics:

  This section will tell you what the NCAA status is for any given school. If you are only interested in Division I schools, check this section.

- Campus Security:

  Unfortunately, security is a real issue on campuses today. This section outlines the extent of protection available to students on a particular campus.

College guides are useful planning tools for you throughout high school because they help you keep in touch with what you will need to enter the school of your choice. Use this knowledge to structure your course selection in grades 9 through 12. In tenth and eleventh grade, use the guides to begin to investigate college offerings. In the college decision process, the guides are essential sources for grounding your search with affordable, reliable, and updated information that is readily available for you to refer to often.

Other Paper Sources

Higher education in the United States is a $150-billion-a-year business, and there are a wide range of publications touting their ability to give you the insider's view on schools and the college entrance process. Some magazines publish once-a-year issues filled with articles and rankings of colleges by comparisons, based on data gathered through responses submitted voluntarily by the colleges themselves. These magazines will give you a general feel for an institution, but they should not be considered definitive. Other books will tell you about making campus visits or writing the application essay or acing the college interview.

Invest your time and money carefully. Check the resources in the guidance department, media center, public library, and local bookstores. Pick up the books and familiarize yourself with what they offer and how they present the information. Which books meet your needs for information? Organize your library so that you have what you need to make the right decisions and can access it easily.

The Electronic Connection

The Internet is a great tool to expand your resources and reach out in ways that were not available just a few years ago. It is a great resource for the initial investigation of colleges, of fields of concentration, or of a particular sport. And it is really great once you have narrowed your list down to about twenty-five colleges. With the help of your guidance counselor, you can get their Web addresses and begin to search their home pages. Even if you do not have an Internet connection at home, many high schools and public libraries have computers with Internet access.

The college search option available on www.CollegeQuest.com allows you to perform your own search using certain criteria. Using this Web site, you can investigate colleges by clicking on the name of the school. This will take you to the college's home page, where you can begin to learn more about it. You can make a printout of the information to add to your folder for that school. Be sure to ask your counselor for feedback on the list of the schools whose information you print off the Web. Check the "College Search Computer Worksheet" (Appendix E) before you begin your search.

One word of caution for the neophyte Web surfer. It is important that you know what information is best retrieved via the Web and what to believe. Since the Internet is unpoliced and is not a secure environment, keep these two points in mind:

- Don't believe everything you read online. Know your source—Is it the official college Web site or a frat house site?
- Be prudent with the information you provide to other users if you contact people through college e-mail directories.

Using a College's Home Page as a Resource

A college's home page can give you a glimpse of campus life that does not appear in the college's brochure and catalog. It is true that the virtual tour will show you the shots that the college marketing department wants you to see and that shows the campus in the best light, but you can use the home page to see other things too.

A QUICK LESSON ON THE ELECTRONIC COLLEGE SEARCH

1. Identify the specific information you are seeking: college information. Keep focused on it so you do not go off on interesting but nonproductive links.

2. Explore the Web with more than one search engine because the subscribers on each may be different and your results can vary greatly. Some excellent engines are Lycos, Yahoo, Dogpile, and Excite.

3. As a rule of thumb, most college Web sites are www.their name.edu. If you can't get to the home page that way, find the area on the screen that says "SEARCH" and type your request. The search engine will provide you with a list of Web sites that most closely match your search criteria. Or go to www.CollegeQuest.com to get links to all of the colleges in alphabetical order.

4. Look at the home page for the icon or picture that leads to ADMISSION and begin your search there. Look for the undergraduate admission link, if there is one, and click on it. Read and print the information. It will tell you everything you need to know to apply to that school. You can also request a catalog, brochure, application, and financial aid information by clicking on the ADMISSION e-mail address.

5. Just for fun, go out on one of the search engines listed above. Type in the college's name and see what hits you get. Is the information different from what the college's home page says?

How long did this whole process take? Can you see how this tool can be an effective time-saver for your college selection search?

- Find the student newspaper. Read the articles. What is happening on the campus? What cultural programs are being offered? What awards and recognition are students and faculty members receiving? Is there any indication that the college and the surrounding city or town ever sponsor joint programs?

- Is there an open e-mail site for students? Read the issues being raised there.

- Go to the department in the major you are investigating. Who is the department chair? Read the biographies of the professors. Does their work sound interesting? What are their credentials? If you have a pertinent question, find the e-mail directory and ask it. Go to the Course Bulletin. What courses are required? Read the descriptions. Do they sound interesting and like things you would be excited to learn about?

- Look up your sport. What is its record? Are there a lot of juniors and seniors who will be graduating and leaving space for upcoming players? Who is the coach? What scholarships are available? What division is it?

- Investigate the student e-mail directory. Is there a student from your high school who agreed to be contacted at this college? Begin a dialogue with him or her about the college. Ask if the contact knows anyone who is majoring in your area of interest. E-mail that person for information, too.

It is generally a good idea to take the information you get on line back to your counselor for verification, especially if the information is new and surprises you. While most sources are reputable, there are some people with their own axes to grind. Besides, it never hurts to have a second opinion.

Computer-Assisted College Search Tools

These are the college search software applications that let you load in criteria and generate a list of colleges. The software allows you to create a standard to compare one school against another on paper. These are wonderful aids for initial fact-finding purposes.

Most guidance departments today have at least one computer-assisted software search program available to students. These programs, like Guidance Informational Service (GIS) or ExPAN®, will take you on a virtual tour of colleges. The form in Appendix E, "The College Search Computer Worksheet," can help you clarify your thinking before you begin the search. Your guidance counselor will ask you how you decided to choose the parameters on the form and will then either help you begin to investigate colleges with the search program or perform a search and compile a list of colleges for you. In a follow-up meeting, the two of you will go over the list in detail.

There is a downside to the computer-generated search software. Sometimes the programs will create lists that include hundreds of schools. If you are not familiar with the software, it can be difficult to know how to use the correct parameters to eliminate or add colleges to your list. You will find that counselors are knowledgeable about the software's ins and outs. Let them help you negotiate your way through this data.

Regardless of who creates the list of colleges, your counselor can use this computer-generated list to provide you with the benefit of her years' of experience and expertise in matching up students with institutions that have compatible personalities. Your guidance counselor will consider such questions as: How have other students from your school done when they applied to these schools? If accepted, did they experience success at these colleges? Did they find the schools satisfied their intellectual and social needs?

You have visited the guidance office more and more frequently. You have hunted the shelves for books on the college application process, explored the files on college brochures and applications, and begun to add college home pages to your "favorite" list. A new blue plastic milk crate, holding colorfully labeled file folders with the names of colleges, sits on the floor of your room waiting to be filled. This is a very good beginning. Now that you have your resources in order, let's talk about identifying schools by the criteria they use to choose their freshman classes.

WHAT REALLY MATTERS?
IDENTIFYING THE CRITERIA SCHOOLS USE

By your junior year of high school, you will probably wonder how you are going to get through this maze of information in time to feel comfortable with your choices. Yes, I said choices. There should be quite a few schools on your initial list because more than one school will meet you on your terms.

Sorting through that list of colleges and making the final list of choices will not be as difficult as you might think. Much of your decision making will be based on facts and objective information. You have already learned how to find reliable resources and search for information. This will be the part of the decision that you will be able to deal with easily.

But there will be other aspects of the decision-making process that are simply intuitive. Some of it works off your subjective feelings about a place—there is no other way to describe the process. It could be something you hear from a returning graduate that turns you off from the school. Or it may be an article that you read in the newspaper that discusses the decaying conditions of a campus. You may visit a school that really seemed to meet all of your desires for size and location, but something the admissions interviewer says or something you hear in conversations with the students on campus convinces you that it's not the place for you.

Both objective facts and subjective feelings will play a part in your decision. How much interplay and impact facts and intuition have varies from one person to the next. One thing that does not vary is the fact that schools have criteria about the kinds of students they are looking for.

The *You* Factor

To understand how you fit into an admissions office's decision about student placement, we need to look at the way colleges categorize their applicants. The following form gives you some descriptions and questions to help you begin thinking in the terms that colleges use to look at students. These descriptions will help you get a better sense of the kind of student that colleges are interested in drawing to their campuses. Understanding this criteria will also help you identify where you might place yourself as you prepare your list of schools and how you might describe yourself on your applications.

After you have read each description and answered the questions, weigh your answers and rate yourself from 1 to 5, with 5 being the highest. See where your strengths lie. Compare them to what the colleges and universities on your list are seeking. Where do you match up? Let the common ground and mutual interests drive your decisions about where to apply.

TAKING AN OBJECTIVE LOOK AT *YOU*

Gathering the following information and filling out this worksheet will help you better understand the admissions process. Having this information handy can also save you time when you complete your college applications.

Academics

Your academic performance is described in number terms only for some university systems, such as the large state universities. Other schools will consider factors such as recommendations from counselors and teachers that describe a student in outstanding scholarly terms. All colleges are looking for an outstanding academic foundation, and it is a strong consideration in their decision-making policies. If your SAT scores are in the 750s and your GPA is 3.8 on a 4.0 scale, you will look like a strong draw to them. Honors and AP courses will also impress them. Remember that colleges would rather see a lower grade in an honors or an AP course than an A in a regular course that did not challenge a student. If your scores are in the 500s and your GPA is between 2.0 and 3.0 out of 4.0, the Ivies and competitive colleges are probably not for you unless you have other talents or mitigating circumstances.

1. GPA (Grade Point Average) _____

2. Weighted HPA (Honors Point Average) _____

3. The honors courses I have taken are:

    English _____

    History _____

    Math _____

    Science _____

    Language _____

    Electives _____

4. The AP courses I have taken are:

    English _____

    History _____

Math _____

Science _____

Language _____

Electives _____

5. Standardized Test Scores

PSAT scores _____

First SAT I scores _____

Second SAT I scores _____

ACT scores _____

SAT II Subject Tests

Test 1 _____ Score _____

Test 2 _____ Score _____

Test 3 _____ Score _____

Rating: (1) _____ (2) _____ (3) _____ (4) _____ (5) _____

Personal Achievement

Remember the recommendation for Josh that you read in Chapter 1? That is what I am referring to here—the type of student who views the world as filled with new experiences and challenges and who thrives on excellence. These are the National Merit semifinalists and finalists, the National Latin Contest winners, and the Cornell Book Awardees. Colleges will line up for these students. But what if your list of achievements isn't quite so illustrious? Write down everything that you have competed in—even if you didn't win. Colleges want to see what interests you and how you have challenged yourself.

1. My academic achievements are _____

_____

_____

2. The level of academic awards I have achieved has been

Local Recognition _____ for _____

State Recognition _____ for _____

National Recognition _____ for _____

3. Overall, I would consider my academic history

  • one of the highest in my class _____

  • average in my class _____

  • at the lower end of my class _____

4. The academic rigor of my high school compared with other schools around the country is

  • one of the top schools in the country _____

  • moderately placed _____

  • average standards _____

  • not an academically competitive environment _____

Rating: (1)_____ (2)_____ (3) _____ (4)_____ (5) _____

Diversity

As part of their admissions goals, colleges attempt to develop a microcosm of society on their campuses. In part, it is what colleges are referring to when they cite a student body that comes from fifty states and forty-two other countries. Colleges include in their definition of diversity the students they draw from Midwestern farms, Southern cities, and New England hamlets as well as from other countries. Colleges want students who come from huge public high schools and from small private academies. They want the sophisticated urbanite who knows the big city experience inside and out and the small-town student who lives next door to her second grade teacher. Coeducational institutions want an equal balance of men and women, if possible. A first-generation college-bound student in a family makes an impression, as does the student from the suburbs whose father is a doctor and mother is a lawyer.

Diversity also mean admitting students that represent all socio-economic backgrounds and a variety of ethnicities, including African-American and various Asian-American groups.

1. Do I have a geographical advantage? (State what it is and with what college[s].) _____

2. Is my ethnic background, which is _____
_____, an advantage?

3. May my socioeconomic background be a factor in my favor?
_____

4. Am I recent immigrant to the United States?
_____

5. a. Am I a male applying to a mostly female institution ?
_____

   b. Am I a female applying to a mostly male institution?
_____

6. Am I the first student in my high school to have ever applied to this college? _____
_____

Rating: (1)_____ (2)_____ (3)_____ (4)_____ (5)_____

Minority and Disadvantaged

Minorities are represented on college campuses in greater numbers today, but ethnicity still plays a role in admissions at some institutions that are trying to encourage a diverse student body. If you come from an African-American; Puerto Rican, Mexican-American, or other Hispanic; Native American; or Asian-American background, you may fall under the federal guidelines in a minority category. Students with physical and learning disabilities may also receive special consideration. You should be sure to note any major adjustments or adversities that you have overcome. Remember the recommendation for Mark in Chapter 2? He overcame a number of problems to become a better student and prospective college freshman.

Private and competitive colleges tend to draw economically advantaged student bodies. However, in recent years there has been an increased awareness among these colleges that students from disadvantaged backgrounds may contribute greatly to their student pool. An academically talented but economically disadvantaged youth from an urban background may bring a unique outlook and set of ambitions to a campus.

1. Do I fit into one (or more) ethnic category? Which?
_____

2. Have I undergone any major adjustments in my life—for example, divorce or multiple relocations?

3. Have I had to overcome any major adversity, such as a physical or learning disability? _____

4. Would my socioeconomic background be considered disadvantaged?

_____

Rating: (1)_____ (2)_____ (3)_____ (4)_____ (5)_____

Athletic Talent

College coaches recruit athletes and are a force to be dealt with in the admissions process. They are after the athlete whose play will make a difference to their team. Alumni of schools where athletics rule can play an important part in recruiting, too. They want to turn on their TVs or travel to a home game and see their team win, especially in football and basketball. But other sports can also lead to an admissions offer and scholarships. The big factor is whether the athlete has the academic equipment to graduate from the college or university after four years. This is the backroom discussion that goes on between the coach and the administration. To some coaches the academics are less important than how much the athlete will help the team. Don't underestimate the influence your athletic talent can have on your college search. Know also that there are colleges and universities that may not be easily swayed by your athletic record.

What if you are not a future football hero? Thanks to Title IX, many colleges have excellent sports programs for women and offer scholarships in sports such as basketball and tennis. (If your tastes run more toward low-key interscholastic competition or even intramurals, that may not get you a second look at a college. But if being able to participate in sports on some level is important to you, be sure you check it out for all colleges that you consider.)

1. In what sports am I lettered? _____.

2. I have been named
   - all county in _____.
   - all state in _____.

3. I have been invited to participate on a national team in
   _____.

4. I am considered an Olympic-level athlete in _____.

5. I have already been approached by recruiters from
   - _____ NCAA Division _____
   - _____ NCAA Division _____

6. Rather than playing on school teams, I have played in local leagues
   and travel teams for _____
   _____.

7. I like the fun of intramural sports and play _____
   _____.

Rating: (1)_____ (2)_____ (3)_____ (4)_____ (5)_____

Special Talent

Do you dance, act, or play the tuba? Creativity and artistic talent are
sought after by many schools, not just to add people to their degree
programs but to improve the quality of campus life. Many schools have
orchestras and bands and produce plays and musicals that rely on the
"amateur" talent of their students.

1. I have performed in various productions inside and outside of the school
   setting. List the titles and roles.
   _____
   _____
   _____

2. I have participated in summer stock or other amateur/professional
   productions. List where, the titles, and roles.
   _____
   _____

3. List any professional experience. _____

_____

_____

4. List any international invitational concerts. _____

_____

_____

5. Am I a member of an orchestra, a band, and/or a chorus? List it/them.

_____

_____

6. I have already been contacted by a faculty adviser from

_____

_____.

Rating: (1)_____ (2)_____ (3)_____ (4)_____ (5)_____

Extracurricular Activities

This area was well covered in Chapter 2, but don't forget that colleges, especially the smaller ones, need students who are willing to perform these responsibilities on their campuses. Make sure you play up your record of involvement.

1. I participate on an extracurricular basis in _____

_____

_____

2. I have held the following offices: _____

_____

_____

3. I have established _____

_____

_____

4. A unique contribution I made was _____

_____

_____

Rating: (1)_____ (2)_____ (3)_____ (4)_____ (5)_____

Leadership/Entrepreneurial Involvement

The first student I met at the last high school I worked at was making more money as a senior in his entrepreneurial venture than I have put together in my whole career. Today, he is a big name in the professional wrestling business—as a businessman, not as a wrestler. Don't underestimate the impact that charismatic personality profiles will have on business schools. They love the movers and shakers. If you're one, let them know it. You may not have earned big bucks in high school, but if you have worked, be sure to mention it. It shows that you have the ability to balance multiple tasks and to be responsible.

Organizers are essential to campus life. They are the leaders who keep it going. Proof that you have accomplished things before will convince colleges that you have a track record that will continue. Not everyone, of course, is going to mastermind an Internet startup, but how have you shown your leadership talent in high school?

1. My entrepreneurial business is _____
_____.

2. Annually I earn _____
_____.

3. I have worked after school and on weekends for _____ years doing
_____

4. I suggested an innovative approach to my employer to _____
_____.

5. I suggested an innovative approach to my school to _____.

6. I have demonstrated leadership in _____
by _____
_____

Rating: (1)_____ (2)_____ (3)_____ (4)_____ (5)_____

Personality

I know when I am in their presence, and so do college admissions interviewers—they are the students with *personality*. Their humor is hilarious, their views on life are unique and filled with vitality, they tell stories filled with vivid details, and their minds take so many interesting twists and turns that you have to be on your toes to keep up with them.

You just want to be around them. Colleges can pick up on your personality during the interview, through the student essay, or by quotes provided in recommendations. Personality just stands out. If you have a really strong personality, look into those schools that give you some air time. The personal interview, as well as peer and teacher recommendations, will be important for you.

Rating: (1)_____ (2)_____ (3)_____ (4)_____ (5)_____

Legacies

Mom is a Dartmouth grad, Dad's a Yalie, your sister attends Berkeley, and your brother is at the University of Virginia. What more could you want? Assuming you want to attend one of these schools and it has the curriculum you are looking for, you have a good chance of being admitted. Legacy goes a long way. Colleges and universities are loyal, especially if your family has been loyal to them. Don't underestimate the legacy role in admissions. Many places in the freshman class next fall are being reserved for members of this group.

I am a legacy at

School 1 _____ through my _____.

School 2 _____ through my _____.

Rating: (1)_____ (2)_____ (3)_____ (4)_____ (5)_____

Use the results to compare your features with those of the colleges you are investigating. What are your most outstanding features? What are theirs? What are you looking for in a college? Who are they seeking? How are you matching up?

IDENTIFYING YOUR CRITERIA FOR SCHOOLS

By now you have your resources in order and are starting to get an idea of how colleges develop a system of placing students by how they present themselves on paper. You're figuring out how colleges might look at you. So let's talk about identifying schools by criteria. Finally, you get to develop a "first list."

Begin by completing the "The College Search Computer Worksheet" (Appendix E) . If your guidance department uses a similar paper tool, use your school's version instead. This worksheet will help you generate your college list. Whether you generate the list with your counselor first or make a start on your own and then talk with your counselor about it, this worksheet will be very helpful. We have talked about the criteria listed on the sheet in our discussions of location, size, and type of college.

The sheet asks you to identify those areas you want to highlight to begin your search. I want to stress that this is a flexible tool. You do not have to nail down all the specifics right from the beginning. There is no harm in developing a list based on some criteria you select in the beginning and then, after exploring the colleges that show up on your initial list, making changes to the criteria and rerunning the search. Think back to the metaphor I used earlier of looking at the college search as a funnel. The goal here is to start the search broadly, with the funnel wide open at the beginning, and then to narrow it by comparing what you are learning about a college with what you are learning that you will need in the college you eventually choose. You will do this by matching your criteria with those of the schools you are looking at.

Trying Your Own Electronic Search

STRETCH: These schools are at the high end or are above your range academically. They are either competitive or admit a small number of students. You are not sure you meet the admission standards, but you should be able to carry the workload.

TARGET: Your scores qualify you for these schools, and you stand a good chance of being accepted. You seem to be in the midrange of other students being admitted to these schools.

SAFETY: Academically you are overqualified for these schools, but they are your safety net.

Now that you have taken a look at the kinds of things colleges will see in you, it's time to take your search on line. If you have not already filled out "The College Search Computer Worksheet" with your information, do it now. Then head to CollegeQuest to start looking at individual schools. If you already have an idea of the schools that you're interested in, do a quick search to find information on these institutions. If you feel like exploring, you can develop a list of colleges based on things like location, difficulty, and majors. Once you have an idea of the schools that match up, you can make side-by-side comparisons to narrow your list, making sure to include safety, target, and stretch schools (you can fill these in on the following chart). After you've done this, you can make a virtual visit to any of the schools on your list by clicking on the school's name. This will send you to the college's home page, where you can begin to learn more about what that school has to offer.

Stretch	Target	Safety

Once you've done this, it's a good idea to make an appointment with your guidance counselor. These Web tools are an excellent resource, but their best purpose is informational. Take the list you developed along with your computer worksheet to your counselor and ask what she thinks of the colleges you have begun to research. Your counselor is really your best resource. Counselors stay current, always looking to the trends of the future and updating their materials. If you want the most accurate data with the human touch attached, see your counselor at this point to help you finalize your list.

NARROWING THE CHOICES TO THE FINAL LIST

How do you finalize your list? You begin by evaluating the colleges. You do that by using all of the resources I discussed in the previous sections of this chapter. You can find many of them in your guidance office. Try college guides like *Peterson's 4-Year Colleges* or surf college Web sites. Begin to refine your research by focusing on things like majors, athletics, retention rates, and facilities.

Order college catalogs and investigate their offerings. How deep are the offerings for the major that you are interested in? If you are looking for a business major, for instance, how many types of business majors does each school offer? If one school has twelve different business majors, everything from accounting to sports business, that is very deep. Compare this school with the others on your list. Five or six is the average number of business offerings at most colleges. The school with twelve majors looks like a strong school for business. Mark with an asterisk (*) any school that is strong in your major area of interest.

Academic Profile of the College

What other factors do you need to rank? As you do your research, look for answers to the following questions about each college's academics:

- How tough is each school to get into? You will need the average SAT and/or ACT scores for each of your colleges.
- How selective is each college? Find the acceptance rate numbers on how many people apply and how many are accepted.
- Do they report the rank of their freshman class? What percentage was in the top 10 percent of their senior class?

College Personality Type

Finding out what type of student each college is looking for will require a little more work. You will need to dig deeper. Look at the categories listed on the "We Match Up" table on page 90. Write in your ratings from the worksheet "Taking an Objective Look at *You*" on pages 76–84. In each of the empty boxes on the top line of "We Match Up," write in the name of a school that interests you.

Fill in the same information for each school that you filled in for yourself. For example, what GPA and standardized test scores does each school say it wants to see on a student's record? What kinds of extracurricular activities does each school offer that interest you? Fill in each column. If you need more columns, use another sheet of paper.

Once you've completed the worksheet, take a look at how you and the different schools match up. Where did you score highest? Look at what these colleges want and where you scored. Hopefully there are a number of matches on your list. As you review the scores, consider questions like these:

- Whom does each school need? Athletes, debaters, certain majors?
- Do students from your state or region seem to have a geographical advantage anywhere?
- Is diversity an advantage with a particular school?
- Is any school looking to balance its gender statistics?
- Look at the application essay topics. Do they tell you about the type of student each school is looking for?

One More Cut

There's still one more factor to consider as you narrow down your list. Go down the list of schools and circle those that your guidance counselor thinks are a good fit for you, if one or both of your parents or guardians like the school for you, if a teacher mentions the school for you, and/or if you want to attend the school.

The Final Cut

Counselors can help you with the last step of the process. Their personal knowledge of the colleges on your list as well as the experience they have had placing students into those schools from your high school and their knowledge of you is at your disposal. It is time to look at your schools in order of selectivity and develop a list with your guidance counselor of your final target, stretch, and safety schools.

As you begin to look at the colleges and whom they want to draw to their campuses and where your interests, academics, and test scores lie, you will begin to see that some of the colleges will stand out. Take your "We Match Up" results and underline those schools that closely meet your needs and wants based on what you have discovered about them. How many of them have been recommended to you or do you strongly feel should be on your list? Mark these with a circle.

Show the list to your parents and friends. Is the information you are basing your conclusions on correct? Does the list need to be modified in any way? Revise your list if necessary as you identify new information. With the help of your guidance counselor, you will be able to narrow the list to a group of schools distributed across all three areas.

What's the Magic Number?

How many colleges should be on your list? It's hard to come up with a hard and fast number, but this much is true—the schools you finally decide to apply to should all be schools you would be excited about attending if you were admitted. As a general rule, your final list should have two to three schools in the stretch area, two to three in the target zone, and two schools in the safety category. Keep the following two things in mind:

- You can continue to make changes to your list. It is not set in stone, and it is *your* list, after all.
- Listen to your inner voice, and trust your instincts.

What's next in the college selection process? The best tool of all to help you determine the match—the college visit.

WE MATCH UP

Categories	My Achievements						
GPA/HPA							
SAT							
ACT							
SAT II/AP							
Academic Awards							
Diversity							
Minority/ Disadvantaged							
Athletic Talent							
Special Talent							
Leadership/ Entrepreneurial Involvement							
Extracurricular/ Community Service							
Personality							
Legacies							
Counselor							
Parents							
Teacher							
Me							

Chapter 4

Touring Campuses

Would you buy a car without seeing it? Of course not. Not only would you see the car, but before you put your money down, you would take several other steps. You would visit various showrooms to find out everything you can about the car you think you might want to buy—colors, features, price, and deals. You would sit in the driver's seat. You would ask yourself a series of questions. What's the interior like? Do you feel cramped or is there enough room? How's the line of vision out of all the windows? If you're 6'3", do your knees fit under the steering wheel? If you're 5'3", is the seat too far back? Some of you would insist on a test drive to see how the car handles. Then you would get out and slam the door to test for solidness—and kick the tires.

Then there's the research you would do. You would buy at least one paperback car book. You would get on the Web and check *Consumer Report* and *Road and Track* magazine for articles on the car. If it's an older car, you would examine the repair history for your model year and the resale value. If "your car" drove up next to you at a red light, maybe you would even roll your window down to ask the driver how she liked it.

It really doesn't take that long to accomplish the car search process. At the end, you will be more comfortable and confident knowing that you took the time to learn as much as you could to ensure that this is the right purchase for you. After all, a car costs a great deal of money, and you certainly don't want to get a lemon.

Makes sense, right? Then how could you choose a college sight unseen?

PLANNING THE COLLEGE VISIT

Did you get the point of my story? Seeing is believing. You may have talked to friends about their college experiences, but they just are not *you.* There is nothing like being there and seeing for yourself. You should try to visit every one of the schools you have decided to apply to.

Don't run out of steam and let this piece go. It is too important. Visiting the colleges is essential to making all the efforts you have put into this process thus far really count. Of all the steps in the process, visiting colleges is the one factor that can make a difference in choosing the right college for you. Think about the time and effort you have put into studying for your academics and how you have "pushed the envelope" when choosing your courses. The alphabet soup of tests was not easy, but you found the time to study and you did well on them. When it came to developing a college list, you started by looking at yourself and asking the hard questions. You tried to determine your real reasons for entering college and found out what you would need from a college to be happy. You have outlined the qualities you prize in a school, developed a college list, researched information about each one, and e-mailed students, admissions officers, and professors. You have done the college selection process well up to now. This is not the time to drop the ball! *You have to leave time to complete this part of your search, and you have got to time it correctly.*

What a College Visit Can Tell You

College catalogs and brochures, videotapes, and CDs do a good job of helping you envision the look of the schools. The virtual campus visits you can do on line or through computer software packages can give you a taste of the flavor of the college or university. But none of them can insert the *you* into the equation. We're all different, and colleges are too.

As any guidance counselor returning to a college or university for a tour after four years will tell you, a school's personality is not carved in stone. Schools change over time. One factor on some campuses is the multimillion-dollar campus building project that generates huge changes. But in general colleges and universities are living entities that shape themselves in response to their "mission." The mission is reviewed and revised, reshaped, and reenvisioned over time by administration, faculty and staff members, and students. As a result, the comments of alumni who have been out of a school for five years or

Ask your guidance counselor for a list of students from your high school that went to the colleges or universities you're interested in and who are willing to talk to prospective applicants.

more need to be considered carefully. That drafty old residence hall may have been torn down and in its place has risen a sleek concrete and glass dorm with every room linked to the college net and a coffee bar on every floor. A great many things may have changed since a grad left. See for yourself!

Colleges love to see prospective students, and they will welcome you with open arms. Because they cannot possibly stuff all the wonderful things they offer into their literature, a campus tour gives schools a chance to show off. If college brochures are a lesson in marketing, the campus tour is a lesson in effective public relations. Schools establish clear goals for the tour and have planned carefully for who leads the tour, what you see, and what you hear. Colleges are delivering a social life on their campus as well as academics, so you should see the range of that social life.

Take your parents with you. The additional insight and their way of viewing things will give you more input. Colleges welcome all ages and like to see younger brothers and sisters on campus—possible future students. The thought of going with your siblings may not make you happy, but this may just be the way it has to be. I will tell you later in this chapter how you can ditch a sibling while you are finding your own way.

Convinced that you have to hit the road and see for yourself? Good!

> **If college brochures are a lesson in marketing, the campus tour is a lesson in effective public relations.**

Making the Plan

Now that you have done your research and decided on a selection of universities and colleges, prioritize them. Decide which ones you want to see first. But how will you know whether or not the school will feel right for you? Obviously, you have to go there and find out. But college is an expensive deal and a big time commitment. You need a plan.

There are a few questions left to be answered before you hit the road. How many schools can I see in one day? What should I be looking for? Where can I get information on where to stay? What do I need to accomplish at the school and in the surrounding community?

How Many Schools Can I See in One Day?

Try not to schedule more than two school visits a day. If you do more than that, you will only be skimming the surface and will not be able to find out the real inside information about a school. (See the section on taking notes later in this chapter.) Set up your visitation schedule so that you are able to see several colleges in the same geographical area during a single session of visits. Five schools is probably the maximum that you can cover in three days. Think about distances, time allotment at each school, and getting from one place to another. Leave plenty of time to travel from one school to another. Road construction can wreak havoc on even the best-laid plans and researched maps.

When Should I Go?

Try to visit when the colleges are in session. After all, you are interested in how your criteria match up with the student body, not the empty buildings. There are certain times in the calendar year when visiting will be the most productive for you. The two most common visitation times are during the spring of your junior year and September and October of your senior year. Some schools offer college visit weekends that are planned around special events, such as the kickoff of a sports season, a ceremony honoring an exceptional guest, or the presence of big entertainment on campus. Sometimes there are weeks when no tours are allowed.

Call the admissions office at each school at least sixty days in advance (120 days is even better), and find out if the school has certain days set aside for touring. Most schools offer a morning and an afternoon tour, Monday through Saturday. This call will also allow you to schedule an appointment with representatives of the school for additional information that you might not be able to get without a personal visit.

Look at the information you have gathered about the college. Does it require an interview? Can you accomplish the interview before or after the tour? (You will find more about the interview later in this chapter.) When you call, ask the admissions office what the appointment schedule looks like, and see when you can schedule your interview. There are other questions you should ask during this phone call. Does the school offer an informational session prior to a tour? What is the schedule for tours? Can the admissions office offer other assistance—

> Some high schools give an excused absence for college visitations; some do not. Check your school's policy. Also look at your holiday schedule. Are there places in the school calendar where you have a Monday or Friday off?

provide transportation from the nearest airport, arrange for overnights, schedule opportunities for you to attend classes?

Whom Should I See?

Even though you will start with the admissions office, there will be other contacts you might want to make on campus. Don't underestimate the importance of a personal connection, but don't be a pest either. If you have a legitimate reason for making the contact, then go right ahead. The admissions office may arrange the contacts for you or may supply you with the contact information. Here are some people you might want to talk with, depending on your area(s) of interest:

- The head coach of an athletic team to find out what positions will be available next year, if freshmen have to play on a JV team, how players balance academics with practice and game schedules
- The theater department chair to determine if an audition is required and how arrangements are made for one
- The fine arts department chairs to ask about portfolio requirements
- The department chair of the science you are interested in majoring in to find out the research area of the department, what publications faculty members and students have written for, whether you could visit the labs

Where Will I Stay?

Next, you need to think about where you will stay, especially if the school is a long distance away from home. You may be able to find out about nearby hotels when you call the admissions office. Failing that, try the city's or town's chamber of commerce, and don't forget the Internet. There are search engines that allow you to check the yellow pages for a list of hotels, airports, car rentals, and even restaurants in most areas of the United States. Also ask your guidance department if it has a copy of *Peterson's Guide to College Visits*. The Rand McNally TripMaker CD included with the book helps you create a set of directions and print a map to coordinate your visit. It also includes information on where to stay in the area. (The *Guide* also contains a listing of colleges and universities with the names of contact people who can help you in planning your visit. Although the book contains information about tour schedules, classroom visiting options, and overnight visits, you will still need to call ahead and confirm details and arrangements.)

When you have all the details worked out, make your reservations. Make them well in advance, especially if you are visiting a campus on a special events weekend.

Making the Most of the Campus Tour

Eventually you will find yourself standing in front of an impressive megalith of education called the Administration Building. Now what? Well, for starters, take a deep breath and head in to the admissions office. Introduce yourself. You are the one who will be going to college, not your parents, so you should do the talking. Take control of the situation.

Ask for a map of the campus. Check in with the contact person who scheduled your visit. While you are waiting, ask for a student newspaper to read later. Ask for a copy of the local newspaper, and page through it. Look for answers to questions like: What are the politics of the community? Do the advertisements and the entertainment-around-town section list anything you would be interested in doing or seeing? Is there a movie theater? What kind of stores does the town have?

Look around the admissions office, too. What kinds of things are displayed on the walls and bulletin boards? How do the staff members treat one another? How do they treat the college students who act as tour guides? Use your time well as you wait for the tour or for your interview.

I have one other word of advice about using your time well: Don't be shy. Make sure that on your trip across the campus you speak to students. Ask about the things that are important to you—classes, teachers, food, security, whatever you want to know about. Ask if there are places nearby to unwind, if the dorms are in good shape, if the labs are well equipped. Now is the time to make sure, not after you are already enrolled!

> **When you go to the admissions office, introduce yourself right away. You are the one who will be going to college, not your parents, so you should do the talking. Take control of the situation.**

The Lone Journey

Most of your questions will be answered on the scheduled tour, but it also pays to do some investigation on your own. Where should you go?

The first place is the Student Center. This is usually the meeting ground for all segments of campus civilization. If there is anything worth eating for sale, this is where you can pick it up. Look around. Who is in the Student Center? Do you see students and professors talking at the same tables? Are people enjoying themselves? Often, student centers provide the venue for entertainment and campus social life. Is there a coffeehouse? A small theater? What can you tell about the school's social life? Again, what is displayed on the walls?

Take a look at the athletic facilities. I have seen some that rival resorts. Sauna, massage room, whirlpool bath, a couple of Olympic-size pools, gym, weight rooms, emerald green playing fields, and an indoor crew boat basin with currents that can be regulated to gale force—college athletic facilities can be quite impressive! Find out how often the facilities are open and whether they can be used by students who are not team members. Check out how far the facilities are from where you will probably be living. Looking at the sports facilities and then at the classroom buildings and labs can also tell you something about where the school places its values.

Make it a point to eat a meal in the dining hall. College dining halls run the gamut from the commercial cafeteria to a private dining room in a dorm. Look around. How does it look? Is it clean? Is it crowded, or is there enough seating? What is the food like, and what do the students say about it? Is the food healthy or is it cholesterol heaven? Is the menu varied enough? What are the hours of operation for the dining hall? Are there meal plans available, and will they work for you?

I said earlier that I would tell you how your siblings could be sent off while you are investigating the campus on your own. Send them and your parents to the Career Center. Explain that you need to split up to make the best use of the time. Here's what your parents should be looking for: How professional are the career placement services? What is the extent of the alumni connection for employment? Do top-notch employers travel to this campus for visitation and recruitment? Does

> You and your parents may feel that the stakes are high during a campus tour, especially if you have an interview set up. Everyone's anxiety level may be elevated. Make a deal ahead of time to be patient with each other.

the school offer internships? What are they like and in what fields? Is the Center run like a twenty-first century establishment, or does everything look like it has been there forever? Tell your parents to take notes for you. After the visit, merge this information with what you learned.

This will sound odd, but I always go behind the dorm buildings to see how many beer cans and empty bottles of liquor are thrown out there. This tells a great deal about the "other" social life on campus, especially when the cans start mounting up by Thursday morning.

While you are looking around, don't forget to ask your questions. Speak to as many people as possible about the classes—are they interesting, too large, more than lecture, or mostly taught by TA's (teaching assistants)? Ask about the quality of what is taught—do students think it is pertinent and career related? Do students feel their majors are well served on campus? How are grades and finals handled? And what kind of student–faculty relationships exist—are they cordial, distant, or mentoring? Even if you talk to students who are majoring in a field totally alien to what you are interested in studying, the information may throw some additional light on what to expect from the school, should you enroll.

The College Visit Note

As a guidance counselor, I have done hundreds of college visits, and after a while, all colleges begin to look like red brick and ivy with huge clocks in the center of campus. The strain of campus visiting, travel, interviewing, and the closeness of the visit to that final decision can make it difficult to remember where you were this morning. Trying to remember information two months from now will be nearly impossible unless you take notes during your visits.

I have included in Appendix C a one-page sheet titled "College Visitation Notes." Make copies and take one with you for each college you are visiting. Fill in the top information before you leave the house so that if you get lost, you will have the telephone number right there to call the admissions office. You should complete all the information during the visit so that when you go back to the sheets later, you will have the same data on each college for comparisons. This sheet will also give you a location to record any new contact information you collect while you are visiting, such as a coach's name and address, and any specific comments a professor makes that you feel are important.

Right after the visit, place the "College Visitation Notes" in the folder you have designated for that school. It will be a useful tool when you are making your final list. It may be that as you read back on your college visit, the notes you made will determine whether you leave the college on your list. Didn't like the feel of the place? Cross it off the list.

Gathering Information

I have indicated a few of the questions you might ask as you walk around a campus and talk with administrators, faculty and staff members, and students, but there are some questions that should be asked and answered each and every time you visit a college. You need to apply the same questions consistently to every college you visit. You will probably think of more that relate directly to your interests and needs. Write them down now on the inside back cover of this book so that you don't lose them. Here are some major questions that should have been answered by the time you finish each campus visit:

1. **Student body:**

    How do I feel? Could I be one of them?

    Gauge how friendly the students are. Did they make me feel comfortable right away?

    Would I feel comfortable among them?

    Are there too many of them—or too few?

    Is there an unspoken school uniform, and is it not in my wardrobe?

2. **Size of campus:**

    Do I feel comfortable here?

    Does the size feel right?

    Where are the dorms located in relation to the classroom buildings? To the Student Center? To the health center? To the athletic facilities?

    Are the rooms small?

    Do freshmen live in separate dorms, and where are they

located?

What's advertised on the bulletin boards in the dorms?

How would I get around campus?

3. **Campus setting:**

Do I like the look and the feel of the campus?

Can I see myself on this campus for four years?

What are the architecture, aesthetics, and layout? Do I like them?

What about the energy on the campus—alive and vibrant or sleepy and restful?

How are the classrooms?

What about that amphitheater—too large?

Are the buildings well maintained? Is the place clean?

4. **Distance from home:**

Am I still comfortable with the distance?

I have taken the drive now. Does it feel too far away? Not far enough?

If I have to take the train or fly, how often can I afford to go home?

5. **Surrounding community:**

Is it what you thought it would be?

Is there enough happening in the local area?

Do the social options offered by the community enhance the choices at this college?

Are there issues between the "townies" and the university community?

If I need to go into a nearby city, how close is it? How accessible is it?

6. **Academic challenge:**

Do I still feel comfortable about being able to handle the academic load?

What do the students on the campus say about the courses and workload?

What kind of time are they putting into their studies?

7. **Special concerns:**

Can this school meet my needs?

Dietary: How do they accommodate dietary restrictions or

religious meal plans?

Students with special needs or handicapped accessibility: What kinds of accommodations will they make?

Long-standing health conditions: Will I be able to receive the services I need?

The Return Visit

Returning to a campus can be helpful when you are down to making a decision about the final two or three schools on your list. For example, a college may remain on the list in second or third place, but the financial aid package it provides makes you want to give it a closer look. This time stay overnight and attend some classes. The admissions office will make the arrangements for you. If you have a contact there from high school, ask to stay on the same floor. Explain that you would also like to attend some classes, especially one in your major area. If you can, plan your trip for a Friday and stay until Sunday, so you can get an idea of what the social life is like on a weekend.

When you arrive on campus, check in with the admissions office. Your contact will have an itinerary arranged for you. This trip will give you the time to ask as many questions of the students as you like and to see campus life for yourself. Prepare in advance the additional questions you need answered.

THE COLLEGE INTERVIEW PROCESS

Colleges have their own interview procedures, and these vary a great deal. Some require an interview on campus; some require an interview with a college representative or an alumnus. Some grant group interviews, and others do not require an interview at all. The more selective a college is, the more likely that it will require an interview. It is wise, however, to have an interview whenever possible.

Why Have an Interview?

An interview is your opportunity to be more than just a stack of papers in the admissions office. It is your chance to personalize the process. Interviews usually do not make or break admissions decisions, but you should try to have an interview at those schools that are of real interest to you and that are realistic choices. If you are one of those charismatic personalities that I described in Chapter 3, the interview will be the ideal place to show your stuff. Interviews also give you a chance to learn firsthand whether a school is a good match, and they allow you to show how interested you are in a school. It is a time to get answers to those questions that were not answered for you in the school's literature.

Most interviews will be informational in nature. In these instances, the interview will be more about your questions about the school than the interviewer's attempt to evaluate you for placement in the college's freshman class. How the interview is conducted and by whom can tell you about the school, too. Is the interview hurried? Who is assigned to participate in the interview process? Is it a senior student employed part-time by the admissions office? Or is it the person who will be reading your folder and who helps to make the admissions decisions?

Interviewing is a lifelong skill, so begin to practice now. Choose the college you care least about and set up an interview appointment there first.

> Be sure to call the college for its policy on interviews. If you can have an interview, schedule it when you make your arrangements for a campus tour.

Arranging for an Interview

Don't schedule your first interview at your first-choice school. You will do better after you have had some experience in an interview situation. Also, try to avoid making your first-choice school your last interview because you want to remain fresh and spontaneous in your responses.

Schedule all interviews well in advance. You might be able to make them part of your campus tours, but this can be difficult with the stress and timetables of trying to pack four or five colleges into a three-day weekend. If the schools you are investigating are far away from home and expensive to travel to, this might have to be your strategy. If for some reason you cannot attend an interview appointment, be sure to call and cancel. A cancellation will not be held against you, but a missed appointment probably will be.

Preparing for the Interview

The interview is a subtle, subjective aspect of the college admission process. You are trying to make a good impression here, so you need to be sincere and polite and show the college that you know something about it and that you have something to offer.

Be sure to read the catalog and write down a list of questions that you want to ask. The interviewer will already have reviewed your information. Take time to think about your strengths and weaknesses and be prepared to speak about them in a positive way. College interviews are not the time for modesty and monosyllabic answers. At the same time you do not want to seem boastful and arrogant. Take stock of the extracurricular activities in which you have participated and your hobbies, volunteer work, and the other ways you spend your time. If there are special circumstances that have affected your life, you may want to address them in your interview. For instance, if you missed a great deal of school because your family went through a grueling year with a divorce, unemployment, or sickness in your family, you may want to talk about it with your interviewer. Take care not to sound as if you are making excuses for yourself, but rather that you are trying to add to the college's understanding of who you are.

You may want to bring a copy of your transcript and your activities resume to your interview. If there is something on your transcript that might need explaining, be prepared to do it. Perhaps getting a B+ in history from a particular teacher was a major accomplishment, but if you are considering majoring in history, a question about this grade might come up. Let the interviewer know how proud you are to have gotten such a terrific grade in this teacher's class and that she made a point of telling her classes that your B+ was only the second one that she has given in forty years of teaching. The first one went to a student who graduated thirty-eight years ago.

Know the time and location of the interview, and plan to arrive early.

Some Questions You Might Be Asked

Try taking a *virtual interview*. Ask a family member or friend to interview you or interview yourself in front of a mirror. Preparing in advance will make the experience more enjoyable for you and for everyone around you because it will dissipate (another good SAT word) some of the anxiety of what to expect.

The questions that the interviewer will ask are meant to draw you out so that the conversation will flow naturally from area to area.

Remember that most college interviews are an opportunity to explore questions that you may have about what the college has to offer you and whether the school is a good fit for you. Mull over the questions listed on the next few pages. Practice elaborating on your answers. Think about the whys of the questions and your reactions to them. Formulate your responses and practice saying them aloud to your family or friends. But don't memorize responses. Your purpose in reviewing these questions is to clarify your thoughts about these subjects, not to write a script.

I have seen many mock interviews demonstrated by directors of admissions during evening parent programs, and I have questioned my students about what was asked during their interviews. The following are some of the most common types of questions asked. An interviewer will ask only one or two of these questions in a category as a springboard to start the conversation rolling. Ask yourself the questions and see what kind of answers you come up with.

Questions About Your High School Experience

The questions an interviewer will ask about high school touch topics about which you are most familiar: your academic background, your thoughts about high school, your extracurricular activities, and your community.

Your Academic Background and School

- Tell me something about your courses.
- What courses have you enjoyed the most?
- What courses have been most difficult for you?
- What is your high school schedule?
- What satisfactions have you had from your studies?
- Has school been challenging? What course has been most challenging?
- Do you like your high school?
- How would you describe your school?
- What is the range of students at your school? Where do you fit in?
- Do you like your teachers? What is your favorite teacher like?
- What do you do in your spare time?
- How did you spend last summer?

- What do you do with any money you have earned?
- If you could change one thing about your high school, what would it be?

Your Extracurricular Activities

- What extracurricular activity has been most satisfying to you?
- What is the most significant contribution you have made to your school?
- How would others describe your role in the school community?
- What activities do you enjoy most outside the daily routine of school?
- Do you have any hobbies or special interests?
- Have you been a volunteer?
- Would you make different choices of activities if you were to do it all over again?
- What do you most enjoy doing for fun? For relaxation? For stimulation?
- How do you spend a typical day after school?
- What do you want to know about our activities?

Your Community

- How would you describe your hometown?
- Tell me something about your community.
- What has been a controversial issue in your community?
- What is your position on it?
- How has living in your community affected your outlook?

Questions About College

The second category of questions is about college. The basic question, one that you should given some thought to when you did your self-evaluation, is why you want to go to college. There are variations on this theme that may come up during the interview. They may cover topics like these:

- Have you worked up to your potential?
- Is your record an accurate gauge of your abilities and potential?
- Is there any outside circumstance that interfered with your academic performance? Tell me about it.

- What is of the most interest to you about our school?
- What is of the most interest to you on campus?
- What other colleges are you considering?
- What do you expect to be doing seven years from now? Twelve years?
- Have you ever thought of not going to college? What would you do?

You and the World Around You

This third category of questions requires some soul-searching on your part. The interviewer does not ask such questions to provoke you but to dig a little deeper into your attitudes and views. This category includes what are generally appreciated as the hard questions. They often include questions about books you have read, a variation on the hero theme, more probing personal queries, and current events topics. The more selective the college, the more searching these questions tend to be. Be sure you respond with your own ideas and enthusiasms. Don't get into a hole by talking about a book you merely skimmed or a topic you are not informed about. Try making up some questions based on these ideas, and give their answers some careful thought.

What About Your Questions?

Take advantage of the opportunity that the interview gives you to ask your own questions. Be prepared with a list of questions that are specific to each school with which you interview. Try not to ask questions whose answers you could have read in the catalogs and brochures.

Questions like the following might prompt some interesting conversation:

- How does the school treat AP scores? Is there a limit on the number of AP credits the school grants?
- What is the system for matching roommates?
- How does advisement work? What is the college's system for course selection?
- Ask about your major. What new offerings are being considered?
- Are any new buildings planned? How will that impact the present look of the campus?

Some Suggestions for a Good Interview

What Should I Wear?

Just as there are costumes for performances, there are interview costumes. For women, a nice skirt or slacks and a blouse, possibly worn with a blazer, or a simple dress is recommended. Shoes should be low to medium heels. Men should wear nice pants with a shirt, jacket, and tie. A turtleneck and sweater or shirt and sweater are also possibilities. Jeans and caps are not appropriate. The admissions areas are professional offices, and it is appropriate to dress for the atmosphere. Although you do not want to give a false impression, this is not the time to make a personal statement about who you are through your dress. If you look around the waiting room and see other potential applicants dressed as though they just got out of bed, it may be that this is their "practice" interview (it is still not a good idea to blow it) or that they are just demonstrating poor judgment.

Managing Your Body Language

Everyone who has ever done interviewing professionally will tell you that something called body language can tell a great deal about a person. Body language is the physical cues that communicate information nonverbally. Interviewers are trained to pick up these signals. How can you send the right message with your body position?

- Sit still and look directly at the interviewer, and if there is more than one interviewer, look at the one who is asking the question at the time.
- Holding eye contact for more than five seconds at a time may be considered by some as intrusive. Others may interpret a person's lack of eye contact as a sign of being shifty or not trustworthy. Try four to five seconds of eye contact, then three to five seconds of looking slightly away, and then back again to making eye contact.
- Do not tap your fingers on the table or the chair arm.
- Do not tap your feet or swing your legs. Sit up straight in your chair with both feet on the floor.
- Breathing slowly and taking time to pause between your thoughts will help you stay calm.

> Treating the personal interview with dignity and respect will create a situation that will be beneficial for you and the interviewer. The most important rule is to be yourself and relax.

Personal Pointers

Here are some additional things to remember.

- Know the time and location of the interview. Plan to be early.
- Have a good attitude about yourself.
- Speak positively about yourself without bragging.
- Be cheerful and friendly.
- Remember that this is a professional setting, so using colloquial language is inappropriate.
- Listen carefully to the questions you are being asked and answer them fully.
- Enjoy the interview. It is a great learning experience, for you and for the person interviewing you

SAYING "THANK YOU"

Campus visits take coordination, and that takes time and effort. The people doing the work are usually in the overburdened admissions department, whcih sets up arrangements for hundreds, perhaps thousands, of students a year. Will sending a thank-you note make the difference between acceptance and rejection? Who knows? But that is not why you are writing the note. You are writing to thank people for making your visit as comfortable and informative as they could.

Thank the admissions office staff. Write to the department chairperson who spent a half hour showing you the classrooms to make it a more real experience for you. E-mail the students you met that night in the dorm who invited you into their rooms, shared their chocolate chip cookies from home, and spent an hour describing their experiences to you. They can be there to welcome you in the fall, and that will make it much easier to get adjusted, won't it? Don't forget to thank your parents or guardians who took the time off from work and underwrote all the expenses. They have been with you every step of the way. Why not let them know how much you appreciate their support?

Applying to College

Applying yourself—think about these two words for a minute.

These two words have several important meanings for you in the college application process. One meaning refers to the fact that you need to keep focused during this important time in your life and keep your priorities straight. These words might pertain to the necessity of knowing the dates that your applications are due and completing the work involved in order to apply on time. Or the phrase might address the issue of who is really responsible for your application.

No one else should be compiling your applications but you. You need to have ownership over the process. The intervention of others in the case of college applications, including the essay, should be for advisement only. The private counselor is not responsible for completing your applications nor should Dad's or Mom's secretary be typing them. Yes, college applications are an additional workload in your senior year on top of those tough academic classes that you signed up for. You will need to make time for your applications along with juggling your college visits and taking those last SATs or ACTs on your testing schedule. You heard from your friends in last year's senior class that this was coming, but you did not fully understand the balancing act senior year can become.

It is so much easier to procrastinate, which drives your parents crazy, so they pitch in to help. It is a strategy that has worked for you in the past, so why give it up now? Because you stand on the edge of adulthood and because you are the one who is going to college next year. They are not going to be there in your dorm room next year to do your work for you. Just how important is the application? In some instances, it will be the only thing about you that the colleges on your list will see.

Chapter 5

ESSENTIAL ELEMENTS OF THE APPLICATION

Doing the applications yourself helps you learn more about the schools to which you are applying. What a college asks in its application can tell you much about the school. State university applications, which are only two pages long and request numbers only, tell you how they are going to view their applicant pool. Usually, they select students based solely on the applicants' GPAs and scores. Colleges that request an interview and ask you to respond to a few other questions or even write an essay are interested in a more personal approach and a different type of student and number of students than the state college is seeking. The topics of the essays can tell you about where a particular school's interests lie and about the school's style and personality, too.

Now that you've done your homework on where you want to apply, you're ready to start thinking about how to do it. That milk crate that you bought to store your materials in has surely come in handy. Catalogs, brochures, financial aid information—it would be all over your bed, on the floor, and in the bottom of your closet. Without an organizing system, you probably would have had to move out of your room by now. But have you looked at this stuff recently?

> Before you start filling out your applications, double-check each school's deadline. This will help you avoid unpleasant surprises later on.

Checking Application Deadlines

I am sure that when you went to college fairs, you collected as much as you could from the college representatives. By now you've probably contacted colleges' home pages on the Web, too, and requested that more information be sent to you. When you visited the colleges, you collected from the admissions offices any materials that you were missing. If all else failed, you mailed a courteous request for information to those colleges you could not reach any other way. (See the "Sample Request for Information" in Appendix D.) As the catalogs and brochures were coming in and you were filing them, did you check to make sure that you had an application for each college on your list? Applications are usually not available until August, so colleges will send you their materials first and follow up with their applications. They keep your name on file if they have sent you an incomplete packet, and they are fairly good about following up. But if you have not received an application by mid-September, call.

You do not want to be at the point of filing applications and not have an application to file for a particular school—not with the waiting time involved to get an application form. It could mean you would have to remove a college from your list because you could not meet its deadline. If you have not done so already, stop and check the dates on each application and on the Common Application. Place the deadlines on your "College Planning Timetable" and on your list of stretch, target, and safety schools. (See Step 3 on page 114.)

Applying On Line

The electronic connection is having a tremendous impact on the college application process. More and more colleges are posting their applications on the Web and informing students of the advantages of applying through this vehicle. In some instances, especially with the large state schools, there can be as much as a three-week time advantage for a student applying on line versus a student applying through the mail.

The Common and Universal Applications

One way around all this paper is to use the Common Application or the Universal Application. The Common Application, available from your guidance counselor, is sponsored by the National Association of Secondary School Principals and is accepted at 190 independent colleges and universities. The Universal Application is available at www.CollegeQuest.com and is accepted by more than 1,000 schools. Both of these forms were developed in an effort to provide students with more convenient ways to apply and to make it easier for students to apply to several colleges at once.

This is a great thing! Think of all the time and energy using a single form will save you. There is no advantage to using a college's own form, so why do it? Parents may have a hard time accepting this concept and sometimes need convincing. Ask your guidance counselor to speak to them about it or have them contact the admissions offices

> The schools that accept the Common and Universal Applications have agreed to review this form of application *with exactly the same weight* as one submitted on their own forms. Use it whenever possible.

directly to check. Either way, they will come away convinced that you do not have to put yourself through the tremendous workload involved in trying to complete individual applications for five or six colleges. Using the Universal or Common Application will help you focus your time and efforts on your academics while allowing you the time to create the kind of application that reflects your best efforts. Here's how it works.

Using their home computers, students fill in their basic biographical and academic information one time, and then submit copies of the application to the schools to which they are applying. Schools that accept these applications treat it with equal weight compared to their own application. By completing the information on one application, students may submit the application to any of the schools listed. Many colleges accept these applications electronically, allowing students using CollegeQuest eApply to submit their applications to any number of schools by clicking their mouse; others require that students print out copies of the Common or Universal Application and send it to them by mail.

Although most schools make their decisions based on these documents alone, there are some that accept these online applications as the first step in the application process. After they receive it, they mail you a supplemental portion for additional information. Expect the supplemental two to three weeks after you submit the initial application. The supplemental may have additional essay questions, so leave time to complete these extra requests. Whether a school requires a supplemental will usually be stated in the description of how to apply to that specific college that can be found in the overview portion of the Common or Universal Application. You should also find this information when you do your research on the college.

GETTING ORGANIZED

Now let's talk about organizing the information you will need to complete your applications to ensure that they are accurate and sent out in a timely manner. Whether you are applying via e-mail or in a paper format, the information asked on all applications is similar. I am going to give you six steps to follow for the successful completion of this part of your college selection process.

Step 1: Practice Copies

Make a photocopy of each college's application that you plan to apply to. Since the presentation of your application may be considered an important aspect in the weighting for admission, you don't want to erase, cross out, or use white-out on your final application.

Make all your mistakes on your copies. When you think you have it right, then transfer the information to your final original copy or go on line to enter it on the college's electronic application. If you are mailing in your applications, try to use a word processor. But if you have to type your applications, make the effort to line up your responses in those tiny spaces. Remember, at the larger universities, the application packet may be the only part of you they see.

Step 2: Deciding on Your Approach

Now that you have the copies, look at them. What information do the schools ask for? Decide how you are going to present your strengths on the application and what approach you are going to use to get your story across. You don't have to use the same theme for all applications, but if you tailor your approach to fit each school's profile, make sure you can support your statements. This is called packaging, and there is nothing wrong with it. It is always important to know who your audience is and to speak in a language it knows and appreciates.

Be memorable in your approach to your application, but don't overdo it—don't mail a castle made of popsicle sticks to admissions offices.

What is it about your application that will grab the admission counselor's attention so that it will be pulled out of the sea of applications on his or her desk for consideration? Be animated and interesting in what you say. Be memorable in your approach to your application, but don't overdo it. You want the admissions counselor to remember you, not your Spanish castle made of popsicle sticks. Most importantly, be honest and don't exaggerate your academics and extracurricular activities. Approach this process with integrity every step of the way. First of all, it is the best way to end up in a college that is the right match for you. Second, if you are less than truthful, the college will eventually learn about it. How will they know? You have to request that support materials accompany your application, things like transcripts and recommendations. If you tell one story and they tell another, the admissions office will notice the disparity—another red flag!

Step 3: Checking on Deadlines

In September of your senior year, organize your applications in chronological order. Place the due dates for your final list of schools next to their names on your stretch, target, and safety list and on your "College Planning Timetable," located in Appendix A. Work on the earliest due date first.

Step 4: Checking the Data on *You*

You need to make sure that the information you will be sending to support your applications is correct. The first thing to double-check is your transcript. This is an important piece because you must send a transcript with each application you send to colleges. Take a trip to the guidance office and ask for a "Transcript Request Form." Fill out the request for a formal transcript indicating that you are requesting a copy for yourself and that you will pick it up. Pay the fee if there is one.

When you get your transcript, look it over carefully. It will be several pages long and will include everything from the titles of all the courses that you have taken since the ninth grade along with the final grade for each course to the community service hours you have logged each year. Check the information carefully. Is everything there? Are your SAT and ACT scores listed? (This will depend on your school's policy; see page 37.) Are the scores correct? It is understandable that with this much data it is easy to make an input error. Because this information is vital to you and you are the best judge of accuracy, it is up to you to check it. Take any corrections or questions you have back to your guidance counselor to make the corrections. If it is a questionable grade, your counselor will help you find out what grade should have been posted on your transcript. Do whatever needs to be done to make sure your transcript has been corrected no later than October 1 of your senior year.

For those of you who have attended local colleges and accrued credits for dual-enrollment programs or other college-level work, you will need to complete the Educational Data Section. It will ask you to

> When you fill out the "Transcript Request Form," be sure to check how much time your high school requires to put together and send out transcripts. To be safe, hand it in well in advance.

list those courses and request an official transcript from that postsecondary institution as well. Your guidance department will help you with the procedure for securing these records.

Now that you have ensured that the information going out from your high school is accurate, you need to make sure it gets to your colleges. Follow up on each transcript request to ensure that it is sent out to reach your colleges by their deadlines. Colleges and universities will usually send you a postcard acknowledging receipt of your materials and noting the information still pending before they can make a determination on your application two to three weeks after you have mailed your application. If you have not received a postcard within three weeks, call the admissions office and verify receipt of your application and materials. Do not procrastinate on this piece by thinking up excuses for not calling—such as you don't want to bother them or they're too busy to look—just do it! Time is slipping by every day!

Step 5: Listing Your Activities

When you flip through your applications, you will find a section on extracurricular activities. It is time to hit your word processor again to prioritize your list of extracurricular activities and determine the best approach for presenting it to your colleges. Some students will prepare a resume and include this in every application they send. Other students will choose to develop an "Extracurricular, Academic, and Work Experience Addendum" and mark those specific sections of their application, "See attached Addendum."

This is a good time to talk about the importance of reading instructions on applications and following directions carefully. For example, the instructions on the Common Application reads in bold letters: **To allow us to focus on the highlights of your activities, please complete this section even if you plan to attach a resume.** The colleges are serious about the directions they give, and failure to follow directions may be one of the reasons an application is not reviewed positively.

If you are a powerhouse student with a great deal to say in this area, it will take time to prioritize your involvement in activities and word it succinctly yet interestingly. Put those activities that will have the strongest impact, show the most consistent involvement, and demonstrate your leadership abilities at the top of the list. This will take time, so plan accordingly. If you feel you have left out important information because the form limits you, include either an addendum or your resume as a back-up.

Step 6: Organizing Your Other Data

What other information can you organize in advance of sitting down to fill out your applications?

The Personal Data Section

Most of this section is standard personal information that you will not have any difficulty responding to, but some items you will need to think about. For example, you may find a question that asks, "What special college or division are you applying to?" Do you have a specific school in mind, like the College of Engineering? Or will you answer the College of Arts and Sciences because you do not know yet in what you want to major? Speak to your guidance counselor if you need help determining which college to apply to at a university. In some universities, there are definite advantages to applying to certain colleges over others. If you are not sure about your major, ask yourself what interests you the most and then enter that college. Once you are in college and have a better a sense of what you want to do, you can always change your major later.

The application will provide an optional space to declare ethnicity. If you feel you would like to declare an area and that it would work to your advantage for admission, consider completing this section of the application.

To complete this section, you are going to need your high school's College Entrance Examination Board (CEEB) number. That is the number you needed when you filled out your test packets. It is stamped on the front of your SAT and ACT packets, or, if you go to the guidance department, they'll tell you what it is.

The Standardized Testing Section

Applications ask you for your test dates and scores. Get them together accurately. All your College Board scores should be recorded on the latest test results you received. Your latest ACT record will only have the current scores unless you asked for all your past test results. If you have lost this information, call these organizations or go to your guidance department. Your counselor should have copies. Be sure the testing organizations are sending your official score reports to the schools to which you're applying.

If you are planning to take one of these tests in the future, the colleges will want those dates, too; they will wait for those scores before making a decision. If you change your plans, write the admissions office a note with the new dates or the reason for canceling.

The Senior Course Load Section

Colleges will request that you list your present senior schedule by semester. Set this information up in this order: List any AP or honors-level full-year courses first; these will have the most impact. Then list other required full-year courses and then required semester courses, followed by electives. Make sure you list first semester and second semester courses appropriately. Do not forget to include physical education if you are taking it this year.

The Cover Letter

You have collected all the pieces of data for the application and are ready to incorporate them into a final product. What else do you need? An individual cover letter to each college or university should accompany your applications. I say "individual" because a generic letter sounds like a generic letter and will not make you any points with the admissions office. Here are some suggestions for what you might include in a three-paragraph cover letter:

- Paragraph 1: Mention what made you choose this college. Was it your campus tour, the courses in your major field of interest, or the location?
- Paragraph 2: Explain what is special about you that makes you and the school a good match.
- Paragraph 3: Tell the college or university how much you are looking forward to joining it in the fall.

Write your letter in such a way that the admissions counselor will be interested in reading further about you.

CHOOSING YOUR RECOMMENDATION WRITERS WISELY

My den floor is covered with piles of paper. To an outsider peeking in through the doorway, it might seem like a disorganized jumble of papers scattered around with no rhyme or reason. But to me, it is a system that works. All the piles relate to a single senior, and they are organized by topic. There is the academic pile, the extracurricular pile, the personal information pile, the honors and awards pile, and the outside interest and community service pile. Then there are the personal notes I have written during the times I have spent with the student that will help me describe this senior in individual terms.

It is November, and like most school counselors across the country, I am immersed in the recommendation writing portion of my job. The weekends and evenings from October through February are spent gathering together data and writing recommendations for my senior students. Many colleges request a counselor's recommendation as part of their application process, but counselors cannot do the kind of job they are capable of doing without the help of their students. That means that you are going to have to provide information and documents that will help the counselor get to know you and write glowingly about you.

The Waiver to View Recommendations

Before I discuss any more about the contents of recommendations, you need to know about another issue that will probably come up—the waiver to view recommendations. It may surface around requests for recommendations and your high school's policy, and it may be part of college applications. The waiver to view recommendations means that your high school or the college to which you are applying asks you to waive your right to view recommendations written about you before they are sent out. Now you may be thinking, "Why would I agree to that?" Schools view waivered recommendations with added weight. The message you send to the school is that anyone writing for you will be writing positively about you and that you are confident that a recommendation written about you is strong enough on your behalf without your intervention. There has been no "prescreening or fine-tuning" by you. The recommendation is the writer's true unedited view. All these factors makes the impact of the content very powerful in the eyes of the admissions committee.

Here's what a high school waiver might look like:

I, with my parents'/guardians' knowledge and consent, agree that all recommendations written by (school name's) staff and counselors remain confidential to all educational institutions and future employers. I understand that I waive my right of access to such information.

Both you and your parents sign.

Speak with your counselor about your school's policy on waivers. Check your applications to see if there is a section requesting that you waive your right to view the recommendations that have been written for you. Since your parents or guardian will have to sign the waiver on your behalf, be sure to explain its purpose to them. If they have concerns about it, have them speak to your counselor or a school administrator. Once a waiver has been signed for you at your high school, be consistent and have the waiver portion on each application signed.

Your Counselor's Recommendation

Back to writing recommendations. In addition to spending time talking with your counselor, there are several other ways to provide information to him or her. Some counselors will give students an essay question that they feel will give them the background they need in order to structure a recommendation. Other counselors will canvass a wide array of individuals who know a student in order to gather a broader picture of the student in various settings. No one approach is better than the other.

Find out which approach is used at your school. You will probably get this information as a handout at one of those evening guidance programs or in a classroom presentation by your school's guidance department. If you are still not sure you know what is expected of you or if the dog has eaten those papers, ask your guidance counselor what is due and by what date. Make sure that you complete the materials on time and that you set aside enough of your time to do them justice.

Some tools that I find particularly useful in providing me with the information I need to write recommendations are the "Autobiography," the "Peer Recommendation," and the "Parent Questionnaire and Descriptive Statement." I add these to something called the "Informal Recommendation" that I ask students to hand out as juniors. Together, these documents give me a view of a student from a few different perspectives.

The Autobiography

If your guidance department does not request an autobiography, ask if your guidance counselor would find this information helpful.

The autobiographical sketch is not busy work, and your counselor is not trying to add to your workload. The questions for the autobiography have most probably been taken from essay questions that various colleges have used on their applications. The activity is meant to help you to prepare responses to similar questions that you may encounter on applications. I have reproduced below some of the questions I use on the autobiographical form I give my students. Read the questions, and think about how you would respond to them.

Your Education

- Which courses have interested you the most? Give two reasons for your answer.
- Which courses have given you the most difficulty? Give two reasons for your answer.
- What do you choose to learn on your own? Consider interests expressed through topics chosen for research papers, lab reports, individual projects, and independent reading; jobs; and volunteer work.

- What do your choices show about your interests and the way you like to learn?
- List one to three books you have read in the last year that are not related to class work. What did you enjoy about each one?
- What has been your most stimulating intellectual or academic experience in recent years outside of school? (e.g., summer experiences, travel) Explain how it influenced your personal growth.
- Do you feel your high school grades reflect your ability? Explain.
- Are there any outside circumstances (in your recent experience or background) that have interfered with your academic performance?

You and the World Around You

- If you have traveled or lived in different localities, comment on those experiences if you consider them significant to your development.
- What do your parents expect of you? Have they expressed specific plans/ambitions and goals for you? How have their expectations influenced the goals and standards you set for yourself?
- What two or three issues in the world distress you the most?
- What activities outside of school have helped you develop better interpersonal skills? Give examples.

Your Personality and Relationships with Others

- What do you consider your greatest weakness?
- What do you consider your greatest strength?
- How would someone who knows you well describe you? Would you agree with the assessment?
- How have you grown or changed during your high school years?
- Which relationship(s) are most important to you and why? Give examples.

If your guidance department does not request that you prepare an autobiography, ask if your guidance counselor would find this information helpful. Whether you provide the information to your counselor or not, it would be helpful for you to write out answers to these questions. You may come across these topics on your applications. If

> If you complete an autobiographical sketch for your counselor, do not limit yourself to what has happened at school. Include experiences and activities from any part of your life, and remember to be specific in your examples.

you take your time and consider your responses carefully in this practice run, you will have the work done when it comes time to fill out your applications. Even if you do not find the same questions, answering these questions may help you know yourself and your interests better when it comes to making the final decision on your college choice.

Peer Recommendation

Peer recommendations are not only a tool for guidance counselors but some competitive liberal arts colleges use them as a way to gain insights into their applicants. As a guidance counselor, I find peer recommendations an invaluable source of perspectives about my senior students that are not available in any other way. Think about it. In many instances, your friends are closer to you at this stage of your life than your family is. You spend many more hours with them in classes, in activities, and in social situations. When I request that students ask for a peer recommendation, I explain that it is an optional tool, and I caution students to choose a friend who is articulate and writes well. The friend should be one who has known the student very well over time and who may be able to share experiences that will provide insights about the student of which others may not be aware.

What do I learn from peer recommendations? I might learn, for example, how much a student has done to help others without ever expecting to receive recognition for it. I learn about a person's people skills and how a student may have given time freely when someone was in trouble. I hear about the hours the captain of the football team put in on his own time to hold extra drill sessions in the summer to help newcomers gain the skills they would need to excel on the team. There is a wealth of this kind of knowledge shared through the eyes of a friend. I treasure the memories that have been retold and the descriptive language used to express the individualism of a friend. These recommendations from friends have helped me write more accurately and personally about my students. Similar recommendations can be an aid to your counselor as well.

> If you are asked to write a peer recommendation for a friend, accept the responsibility. Your comments will be valuable to your friend, and you will gain an appreciation of what goes into writing a recommendation for someone.

The following are some questions I ask my students to think about as they write peer recommendations. I encourage them in answering the questions to cite those examples that have shaped their feelings toward their friend.

- How long and in what context have you known the student?
- Why do you value knowing this person?
- What do you feel are this person's strengths and weaknesses?
- Does this person possess any special talents or abilities?
- What qualities do you feel this person will bring to a college campus?

Your Parents' or Guardian's Input

The "Parent Questionnaire and Descriptive Statement" is an area where your parents can portray their images of you and tell their stories about how you have matured. Parents' views are usually fairly accurate. The experience of "putting your child down on paper" is a poignant one for parents and often prompts touching conversations between parents and their maturing son or daughter. This is a difficult time for parents because separation and distancing are a necessary part of this process. Don't be impatient. Taking the time to honor their feelings is important.

The following are some of the questions I use on my "Parent Questionnaire and Descriptive Statement." Reviewing them will give you an idea of what your guidance department may ask. Share this information with your parents or guardian so they can be prepared.

- In which areas have you witnessed the most development and growth in your child over his or her high school years?
- What are your child's outstanding personality traits?
- If you had to describe your child using five or six adjectives, which ones would you use?
- Have there been any unusual personal circumstances that have affected your child's educational experiences or personal development? Please explain.
- Please describe your child in terms of achievements in school. What anecdotes can you provide to illustrate the qualities you

most admire about your child in the school setting? What example would you use to describe your child at his or her best in this setting?

- Please describe your child as a person. What qualities do you admire? What anecdotes might illustrate your child at his or her best outside the school setting?

- What would you most like a college admissions officer to know about your child?

Informal Teacher Recommendations

Besides the formal teacher recommendation, which I will talk about next, some schools may use a system of informal recommendations. The purpose of informal recommendations is to provide your counselor with a more inclusive perspective of who you are. Colleges do not see these.

The informal recommendation form is often distributed to teachers in students' junior year to be returned to the guidance department. Through these recommendations, your counselor will see how teachers are thinking about you. Their comments will help the counselor identify your strongest academic areas. When writing his or her own recommendation for you, your counselor can incorporate ideas and quotes from these recommendations, which enables the counselor to present a broader academic and personal view of you to the college.

Rather than sending a form to teachers to fill out, some schools ask at the end of the school year that all teachers post a comment in students' cumulative folders for each student they teach. Ask your guidance counselor what your school does.

Formal Teacher Recommendations

In addition to the recommendation from your counselor, colleges may request additional recommendations from your teachers. Known as formal recommendations, these are sent directly to the colleges by your subject teachers. Most colleges require at least one formal recommendation in addition to the counselor's recommendation. However, many competitive institutions require at least two, if not three, academic recommendations. Follow a school's directions regarding the exact number. Too much paper can dilute the strength of your application.

> Writing recommendations along with their regular teaching load puts a strain on your teachers. Be sure and secure your formal recommendation writers early in your senior year. Give your writers plenty of lead time.

Check with your counselor about whether to supply any additional recommendations based on your unique circumstances.

Recommendations are looked upon by colleges as an important factor in their decision making, and a detailed recommendation can make a favorable difference in the college admission process. Do not underestimate this portion of the application. Choose your recommendation writers wisely. You will request formal recommendations from your teachers as a senior. How do you go about requesting a teacher's recommendation? What should you consider in selecting a writer?

One concern you may have in selecting writers, especially in light of the waiver to view recommendations, is what if you ask a teacher for a recommendation and he or she writes something less than flattering. This is unlikely. You are going to approach your recommendation writers personally to request that they write for you. You may be met with a polite refusal on the order of "I'm sorry, but I'm unable to write for you. I've been approached by so many seniors already that it would be difficult for me to accomplish your recommendation by your due dates." This teacher may really be overburdened with requests for recommendations, especially if this is a senior English teacher, or the teacher may be giving you a signal that someone else may be able to write a stronger piece for you. Either way, accept the refusal politely, and seek another recommendation writer.

How do you decide whom to ask? Here are some questions to help you select your writers:

- How well does the teacher know you?
- Has the teacher taught you for more than one course? (A teacher who taught you over a two- to three-year period has seen your talents and skills develop.)
- Has the teacher sponsored an extracurricular activity in which you made a contribution?
- Do you get along with the teacher?
- Does the college/university indicate that a recommendation is required or recommended from a particular subject area instructor?

- If you declare an intended major, can you obtain a recommendation from a teacher in that subject area?
- TIP: Provide recommendations from two subject areas (e.g., English and math).

A word of advice: Your recommendation writers need to be covering fresh ground. When you ask your teacher or guidance counselor to write for you and they ask for a copy of your resume, tell them you are

---

Making it Easy for Your Recommendation Writers

Organizing the materials for your recommendation writers will make it easier for them to complete their letters on time and will earn you their thanks. It may even contribute to how glowingly they write about you.

1. Provide each teacher with a pocket folder with your name on the front.
2. Include in each folder the following:

   - A list of the schools you will be applying to with the application deadline date for each college.
   - A stamped and addressed envelope for each college to which you are applying.
   - If the college application includes a teacher evaluation form, clip the form to the envelope you addressed for that particular college.
   - If an application does not include a teacher evaluation form, clip a note to that addressed envelope saying, "There is no teacher evaluation form for XYZ college. Please send a recommendation letter."

3. Clip a note to each college packet with the due date for the application so the writer will know when the recommendation must be completed and mailed to the college in order to arrive in time.
4. Write a thank-you note to each teacher and put it in that person's folder. It can be short, but it should be appreciative of the time the person spent in writing the recommendation for you.

---

already sending a copy of it with your application. There is nothing more counterproductive than to hand an admissions officer the same kind of information over and over in different formats. Offer to set up an appointment with your recommendation writers so that they can get to know other aspects about you. When you meet with them, make sure you have your parental questionnaire and peer recommendation in hand.

Other Recommendation Writers

This is the time to talk about the "other" suggestions that you may get for recommendations: your employer, your rabbi or pastor, the director of the summer camp where you worked for the last two summers, and so on. Unless these additional letters are going to reveal hidden pearls of wisdom about you that will have a profound impact on the way a college will view your candidacy, be very careful about overloading your application with too much paper.

This is the time to be highly selective about what information you are including. The pieces of an application should be used to create a picture about who you are. Redundancy is a waste of the admissions officer's time. Your counselor will not repeat academic information that is part of the transcript. Instead, he or she will craft a recommendation to fill in the blanks about you as a person and member of the community. Are there any "blanks" that only other people could legitimately fill in?

One other note of caution is important here. Another area where you may need to deal with well-intentioned but potentially harmful suggestions has to do with offers "to make a call for you." What do you do about the suggestion that you might get from a business partner of your father who says he could help your candidacy by making a phone call for you? After all, he did graduate from the university nineteen years ago, and they will remember him. Unless he has contributed enough to this university's building fund to have a library named after him, decline the offer gracefully. I am being facetious here, but unless the relative or family friend has had an ongoing and committed alumnus relationship with the institution, it really may not be useful to agree to the offer. You may receive some pressure here, so it would help to speak with your parents before these suggestions are made. Then you and your team will be in agreement about how you will respond.

The pieces of an application should be used to create a picture about who you are.

You have chosen your recommendation writers with careful thought and consideration. You have placed everything they need in their hands to accomplish the task. Now it is your turn to write. Did I just hear you groan?

WRITING THE PERSONAL STATEMENT OR COLLEGE ESSAY

The deadline for mailing your application is tomorrow by midnight, and you are just now sitting down in front of the computer to write the "Personal Statement," or college essay, portion of the application. What's the rush, you ask. After all, your English teacher and guidance counselor can look it over tomorrow in school and make suggestions. That will leave you plenty of time after school to make revisions and get it in the mail by midnight. Hmmmm. What post office is open at midnight to postmark your envelope?

> The essay is an opportunity to demonstrate just how unique you really are. Someone is going to take the time to read about you because who you are matters to them.

This is an exaggerated picture of a senior facing the college essay, but in reality your parents have probably been asking you for weeks how far along you are on it. You have managed to duck them when they tried to nail you down. Don't they realize that you have been constructing it in your head all this time, that you will be able to sit in front of the computer and after an hour pull out an essay just short of perfection? The way they are acting, you would think your future depended on it.

If you are thinking "Yes, that's probably how I would do it," let me say that this is *not* how you should do it.

The Importance of the Personal Statement

Why are colleges asking you to write the Personal Statement anyway? Whether it is a single essay question you are asked to respond to or several thematic essay questions like those on the Bowdoin application, colleges are using this approach to learn more about what kind of a person you are and how well you can use the written word to communicate your thoughts.

It is called a "Personal Statement" for a reason. This is an important concept to grasp from the start. Colleges are not looking for a chronicle of your life, and they do not want to be bombarded with so many facts that they feel you are writing "away from yourself," distancing yourself from your topic. Colleges want to know how you *feel* about whatever it is you choose to write about. They want to hear your personal perspective about the topic.

It is true that there can be some anxiety involved in writing about your thoughts and feelings. Some anxiety? The essay can generate a great deal of anxiety because you are being asked to put a piece of yourself down on paper for others to see. In this case, that piece may be a determining factor in the decision to admit or not admit you to the school of your choice. It is a weighty piece of the application process staring at you, and it is all in your hands. It is no wonder that high school seniors complain so loudly to their friends about the college essay and procrastinate before they get down to finally writing. How do you write about yourself? What part of you do you talk about? What part of your life is the most important to highlight?

In the end, writing the college essay is all about attitude, keeping a positive view about the experience of writing the essay and seeing it as a great opportunity. This may be the first chance you have had to look back on your life and consider all the wonderful things that have happened to you (could be a topic here) and all the great people who have come into your life and shared their experiences with you (another question often asked in essays). Most students I have spoken with after they have written their essay believe they have come out of the experience changed in some way.

Eight Building Blocks for the College Essay

Let's make this opportunity work for you. I offer you the following words of advice culled from sessions offered every year by directors of admissions to audiences of parents and students. The faces in the audiences change every year, but the basic elements of a good Personal Statement don't.

1. **Start with yourself.**
   Begin by preparing your resume and a list of your activities. Take

time to appreciate just how special you are and how much you have done to get to this point. Look at what your strengths are. Make sure these strengths are covered in your application. Ask yourself: "Where else in the admissions packet are my strengths discussed? Are they included in my resume? Is someone covering it in a recommendation? Does the transcript highlight this information?" Know your supporting materials, and become familiar with the type of information that will be presented in every accompanying document. If something is not covered in that way, should it be part of your essay?

2. **Deal with the way you look on paper.**

   Your high school record is there on paper. Your transcript will reflect your grades and the quality of the courses you have taken and are taking. This is the time to look at yourself on paper. Are there circumstances that have contributed to a poor grade, or was there a time when you excelled in the face of particularly difficult circumstances? The essay may be the vehicle you can use to address these circumstances.

3. **Cover new territory.**

   Don't be redundant. Your courses are on your transcript. The schools will receive your SAT scores and/or your ACT results. The essay is not the place to list your courses. What is new that needs to be said about you?

4. **Own the Personal Statement.**

   The essay is your place to shine. Colleges are asking to get to know you on a personal level—you need to let them in. Here is your chance to develop a part of your application that is uniquely you. Remember: You own this section.

5. **Write in your own voice.**

   There should be no question in anyone's mind about who wrote the personal statement. It should be in your voice. Many colleges include a request for a "graded sample" of essay writing from their applicants. This policy began when it became apparent that some candidates were paying others to write their essays. If your

English grades are Cs and you scored 423 on the Verbal section of the SAT, an essay that is the equivalent of a Shakespearean play will raise some eyebrows. If you have been hiding this talent all these years, an astute admissions officer is going to ask why.

6. **Make them see it through your eyes.**

   Show the admissions committee what you mean. Don't bore it with a long, colorless recitation of a tale. Make your story come alive for them and have them experience it through active writing. Create interesting characters and vivid scenes. Use an active voice and sensory words.

7. **Presentation counts.**

   If you are not applying on line, use a word processor if at all possible. (This is true for the application, too.) If you are entering your application on line, be sure to write your essay, revise it, and proofread it as well as get the opinions of your English teacher and guidance counselor before you start filling in the online template with the final copy. Don't just write an essay and click *Send.*

8. **Write it now!**

   Your parents are not getting any younger, and each one of those gray hairs on their heads has your name on it! Seriously, you just may surprise yourself with how much you have to say when you finally sit down to write your essay.

Some Possible Essay Types

There are certain common themes in most college essays. You can expect to see a question asking you to evaluate a significant experience or achievement that has special meaning to you. Or you may be asked to discuss some issue of personal, local, national, or international concern and its relation to you. Another question might be to indicate a person who has had a significant influence on you and to describe that influence. These are standard questions and are included as options in most applications. I say *options* because some schools will require more than one essay. Thought-provoking and often entertaining, these questions are developed to probe the way your brain works.

Putting It All Together

Get started by creating a self-outline. Try some of these ideas to begin putting your ideas on paper—or the computer screen.

First, you need ideas:

- Brainstorm: set a time limit or fill a page.

  - everything you can think about yourself—good, bad, special, obvious habits
  - things done, places visited, accomplishments you are proud of
  - sayings you have heard around the house all your life (Could these be used as a theme in some way?)

- Keep a journal for a couple of weeks, recording not what you do but your responses or thoughts about each day.
- Collect important moments from your past.
- Use your resume as a springboard for ideas. Over the course of several days or weeks, ask yourself

  - what your strengths and weaknesses are. Be totally honest.
  - why you do the things you do and what you care about.
  - what it is like growing up where you do.

Once you have your ideas, focus

- Make connections. Group together similar ideas or events, for example, volunteer projects and love of science
- Focus on four or five important strengths. Keep the unusual and vivid ideas from your self-outline, and always be positive!

Next, prove it

- The purpose of the essay is to persuade, so you will need to prove your points.
- List personality characteristics and five or six pieces of evidence about what you have done and who you are.

Try not to make an essay fit a question just because you do not feel like writing another essay. This part of the application process is going to take time, and it will not be easy. There are those very selective colleges that are ingenious in the way they ask their questions. They want to see the same creativity and ingenuity in the responses to their essays. Questions like these will really challenge even the most elastic minds. You do get a choice and pick of the standard options, but think about the question for a minute or two.

Writing the Essay

You have probably been using the writing process since you were in middle school to brainstorm, draft, write, revise, and polish your writing. It should be second nature to you by now, so use it to write your essay. I have already given you some suggestions for brainstorming ideas. Use them to create your first draft, focusing on the content to communicate your thoughts. Then set it aside for a day or two. When you reread it, you will have a fresh perspective. Make any necessary revisions. This is also the point at which you should consider matters of organization, style, grammar, mechanics, spelling, and tone. Once you have rewritten your first draft, you may wish to try it out on your family, friends, English teacher, and guidance counselor. While the final product and final voice should be yours, these people may be able to offer helpful suggestions for technical improvements. When you are satisfied, add it to your application.

Some Dos and Don'ts

Within this general outline for writing your essay, remember these "dos" and "don'ts":

Do

- Leave plenty of time to revise, reword, and rewrite. You can always improve on your presentation.
- Think "small" and write about something that you know about.
- Reveal yourself in your writing. It is OK to talk about your anxieties or a very difficult time in your life. If you do, speak to how you grew because of this experience.
- Show rather than tell by giving examples and illustrating your topic. This approach will help bring your story to life.
- Write in your own voice and style.
- Read the directions and follow them carefully. If they say limit your statement to 500 words, they mean it.

- Remember to link yourself to the college for which you are writing this essay. Write different essays for different colleges—that is, you may use the same general theme, but be sure to include how you and a particular school match up.

Don't

- Write what you think others want to read.
- Exaggerate or write to impress.
- Use a flowery, inflated, or pretentious style.
- Use clichés.
- Neglect the technical part of your essay (grammar, mechanics, spelling, organization, and sentence structure).
- Ramble. Say what you have to say.
- Handwrite your essay. Whenever possible, type or use a word processor.

Write a real essay, written by a real person. Dig deeply inside yourself and speak from your heart, with sincerity and seriousness of purpose. Let the admissions committee see who you are and what you are really about. When you have finished your essay, you will see how mature you have become. It may impress you, and it will certainly impress your audience—the admissions committee of the college of your choice.

EARLY ACTION AND EARLY DECISION

No other area in the college admissions process has received as much attention in the last few years as the use of Early Action (EA) and Early Decision (ED) options as strategies for entering the Ivy League and highly competitive colleges. No other area is as surrounded by misinformation, hysterics, and misuse. Statements like these shed light on the pressures being brought to bear on the college admissions process and, in turn, such statements heighten the pressures:

1. Top candidates are being rejected by the Ivy League and highly competitive colleges of their choice, and applications to the less competitive and state universities have increased.
2. The process of applying to college has become more and more competitive every year.

3. Increased numbers of students are choosing college after high school graduation. About 67 percent of all high school seniors go on to college.

4. The culture in suburban communities demands that children in those communities plan to go on to college after graduation, with the result that 70 to 80 percent of them are entering college. The expectation is that these trends will increase over the next ten years.

5. Excellent college advisement has become available to a broader range of students, not just those in affluent private and public high schools. The consumer has become more knowledgeable and sophisticated.

6. Students with SAT scores of 1450, 5s on their AP exams, and honors courses on their transcripts who excel in leadership, extracurricular involvement, and community service inside and outside of school are being rejected or wait listed by schools like Harvard, Brown, Georgetown, and Wesleyan.

Fewer spaces mean more competition. What do you do to beat the system? Many students are taking the route of Early Action or Early Decision plans.

The Early Options Controversy

EA and ED can be valuable tools for students who know for sure which school they want to attend, but it is not always the best answer. To decide whether EA/ED is a good solution for you, you need some facts and accurate information. First, we need to define the difference between Early Action and Early Decision. Under the Early Action Plan, a student applies to a school early in the senior year, between October 30 and January 15, and requests early notification of admission. The decision usually arrives within three to four weeks after application. If a student is accepted, there is no obligation to attend that institution. The student can bank this admission and still apply to other colleges during the regular admission cycle. Under the Early Decision Plan, a student applies to an institution early in the senior year, also between October 30 and January 15, and requests an early notification of

> Agreeing to abide by an Early Decision is a binding obligation. You may change your mind, but you can't change your signature.

admission. But with this plan, the student and his or her guidance counselor sign a contract at the time of application which indicates that if accepted, the student is obligated to attend that institution. Some schools offer both EA and ED options.

So why has this turned into a controversy? Over the last few years, stories about highly competitive but limited admissions have led students to use the early option in an attempt to ensure a place in their first-choice school because they fear that all the slots will be gone if they apply through regular admissions. Counselors and parents have often had to deal with the fallout from students using the early option as a timing strategy for assured admission.

It has become so big an issue that the National Association of College Admission Counselors bulletin sent out a plea to colleges entitled *Counselors Need More Information about ED/EA from Colleges.* The NACAC asked colleges to share their thinking and their policies on early options with counselors so that we would be in a better position to advise our students about questions such as: Are my chances for admission better if I apply early? Will an early decision affect my financial aid package? What if no one accepts me for Early Action? No one seems to be asking how many students schools actually accept through EA/ED.

Because the timing of applications has become an admissions strategy, schools that had never considered offering an Early Decision or Early Action plan have instituted one or both options. Other schools have changed from Early Action (the nonbinding option) to an Early Decision Plan. Some colleges are offering two calendar dates for their early options, one usually around November 1 and the other in January, to entice strong candidates who may not have gained entry into their first-choice stretch school and who would like the advantage of being considered under an Early Option at another choice.

The Advantages of Applying Early

The obvious advantage is that you will know in December whether you are admitted, denied, or deferred. If you receive a thick envelope, you can relax and truly enjoy the challenges and experiences of your senior year. Make the most of it! If you receive a thin envelope, you will have

> **A deferred admission means that the school is interested but cannot admit you at this time. You can take advantage of the interval between December and April to add to your file in the admissions office.**

to come to terms with your disappointment and then move on. Complete your other applications and wait for April's decisions. A deferred admission means that the school is interested but cannot admit you at this time. You can take advantage of the interval between December and April to add to your file in the admissions office. You might send a notice of an award or special recognition that you have received. Also, play it safe and submit your applications to the other colleges on your list.

Are there other advantages? Overall, most colleges and universities do not believe that there is an advantage in applying early as a strategy to increase the prospect of admission. Colleges say they try to make the same decisions in December that they make in April. As the Director of Admissions for Brown University noted recently, "The acceptance rate for Early Action applicants tends to be slightly higher, but that is because the pool is slightly stronger with highly qualified applicants who have carefully considered colleges and assessed their suitability."

That last clause is important. If you are going to apply for EA/ED, you need to be sure that you are applying to the right match for you.

Johns Hopkins University in Baltimore has the following philosophy about early option applicants, which echoes many other schools' view. Hopkins believes that applicants for early decisions demonstrate a strong commitment to the school. A student who seeks early admission sends a very clear message that the student wants that particular school. If a typical student in the regular application pool has an A average, the average in the early decision pool may be only A- to B+, but these students show definite interest in the school, which weighs in their favor at decision time.

The Reality of Early Options

Don't apply early just because magazine and newspaper articles claim that all the spots in all freshmen classes across the country are taken by early applicants. If you investigate the colleges of your interest, you may find that the reality at the schools on your list does not support such statements. Overall, there has certainly been a growth in the number of early applicants, and schools are admitting more people early. However, the number is far smaller than you would expect from the media.

Schools are interested in students applying early only if they are well matched for the institution. As the Director of Admissions at Brown advises: "If you are unsure, then wait and investigate other options. Do not feel pressured to apply early in the hope of enhancing your chances for admission. Since colleges have so many good applicants in the regular pool, they must be careful not to use up all of their places early. They want the best students to be at their institutions, whether you apply for early action or for regular admission." It is essential that you explore the outcomes and statistics of the Early Action or Early Decision plans at the schools you are considering. It is important to know the truth about their early acceptance rates.

When Might an Early Option Be Appropriate?

Under certain circumstances, it may be appropriate to consider early options. However, early options should not be used as a way to try to get into a college that is way off the chart of possibilities, above even your "stretch schools," based on your course load, GPA, and SAT/ACT scores. Early options might be a consideration under the following circumstances:

- You began your academic planning for high school early and have been successful in choosing courses that challenged and pushed you to gain knowledge.
- You have managed to achieve academically in those challenging courses, maintaining a high standard in all your classes.
- You familiarized yourself with the college exploration process early on, identifying who you are and matching yourself to colleges that offer a program that meets your needs.
- Through accessing advisement, researching resources, and attending informational sessions, you have identified those specifics about college offerings that are most attractive to you.

- You arranged your college visits to get a real flavor for the colleges on your exploration list. You returned to those you found most interesting and attended classes and stayed overnight.

- There is an exact match for you at one particular college. You feel you would be successful in that setting and that the academics and the school's approach to learning meshes with your learning style. The campus environment and personality of the student body make you feel at home, and you can see yourself there for the next four years.

- Your statistics are in the range for this school. It may be a stretch school for you, but you would be able to handle the academic demands at the institution.

- You would not have a second thought or regret about the other colleges on your list if you were accepted early to this "first-choice" college.

- You are not in the position where you need to review the financial aid package from several colleges to compare which package offers you the most money.

- This really is your first-choice school.

Choices are always good to have, but understanding all the pieces that go into the choices is even more important. Before choosing an early decision/action option, speak to your counselor. Don't forget that you and your counselor must sign the statement on the front of the application if you are taking the Early Decision option. The statement will tell your counselor to sign only after he or she is sure that you understand that this is a binding decision on your part. Explore all your options and the facts with your counselor and your parents or guardian before signing.

ROLLING ADMISSIONS

Another option that you may have is the Rolling Admissions Plan. There is no deadline for filing the application. This concept is most often used by state universities. Students receive their letters within three to four weeks after they submit their applications.

Rolling applications are processed for consideration as they are received. Although standards generally remain constant throughout the application period, the number of openings steadily shrinks as offers are made. That means that if you wait too long—even though the application deadline has not passed—it may be harder to get in.

If you are planning to apply to out-of-state public universities, it is best to apply as early as possible. These schools hold open very few slots for students who do not reside in their state. For the more selective out-of-state universities, you should submit your applications to your guidance department for completion as early as October 31. That means that your testing should be completed by then and that your test scores are in the range for these universities.

Once you receive your acceptance, you may still complete applications to other colleges. It can be a relief, though, to know that you have a place in a college or two on your list. This gives you some breathing room to pour your energy back into your academics.

ADMISSIONS DECISIONS

If you developed your list using the practices discussed in this book, you have applied to a range of schools. The only official letters that you will receive will come from the Director of Admissions. While it is thoughtful for the coach or department chair you have been communicating with to send you a letter indicating that you have been accepted, the formal admission letter must come from the Director of Admissions. What might such a letter say?

There are several terms used to describe the decisions made by admissions committees: admit, admit/deny, deny, and wait list. What admit means is fairly clear: you are in! Admit/deny means you have been granted admission but denied financial aid. But the other two categories require some discussion.

The Wait List

To be wait listed means that you are not in yet but have been placed on a waiting list in case an opening becomes available. Schools rank the applicants from the regular admission pool on their waiting lists in

For full definitions of these and other terms you might encounter in the college entrance process, see the Glossary.

order of priority, and unfortunately the more competitive schools have years when they never draw from their wait lists. After a while, a rejection notice is sent, but you must be notified by August 1.

Wait-list decisions are difficult, especially if you have applied to an institution and have not processed any other applications in the interim. This is another reason to use caution when deciding to "go early" on an application. Some students will lose their motivation to continue to do the work for their other applications once they have received a wait-list decision. It may take some remotivating and several late-night conversations with family and friends to get refocused, but it is important to get those other applications out. I suggest to my students who decide to submit an early application that they continue to work on their other applications and have them ready to mail if the need arises.

If you receive a wait-list notice on an early decision, remember that your application has been returned to the regular pool to be reviewed during the next cycle. If you are wait listed during a regular admissions cycle, you are placed on a ranked wait list. According to the NACAC's "Statement of Students' Rights and Responsibilities in the College Admissions Process," you have the right to a history of that school's wait list that indicates how many students have been on the wait list, how many were offered admission, and the possibility of housing and financial aid for those students who were later accepted. Your counselor can help you with this by making a call to the admissions officer who has been responsible for your file.

> Check the NACAC Web site, www.nacac.com, for the full text of "Students' Right and Responsibilities in the College Admission Process."

Either way, it is important to keep the college that wait listed you updated on everything new that would add to your application. Academic milestones, projects, awards, or outstanding achievements should be communicated. Letters from your teachers highlighting special projects that you may have participated in during this term can be helpful. Ask your guidance counselor to coordinate the efforts so that the college does not feel bombarded and pressured but continues to feel informed and reassured of your continued interest in it.

The Deny Decision

Occasionally, an application that seemed to be well placed for a "yes" at a particular university is denied. Sometimes, factors may be involved in admissions decisions that have nothing to do with the qualifications of the applicants. For example, yearly goals are set by the administration of every college and university in the country, and admissions policies are then established to meet these goals. Suppose a particular college had an outstanding yield for last year's freshman class. This means that the number of students who accepted admission to that school was higher than usual. A high yield may cause difficulties for a college or university, especially when dormitory space is limited. The school may not have had enough space for all the students who entered in the fall. As a result, a decision was made to admit fewer freshmen this year to bring the numbers back into line.

What effect will this decision have on you if you decide to apply to this college this year? You will find that the standards for entry will be higher and the number of students who will be admitted will be less. The guidelines for admission that you researched for this particular school were accurate for every year but this one, and you may not know about this policy until after you have received your decision. The deny decision had less to do with you and more to do with the situation at that college. Things like this go on all the time at universities, so do not take the decision personally.

These "unknown" circumstances are part of the reason to develop a list that offers options in the stretch, target, and safety zones. The aim is to end with several colleges to select from in all three areas. There may be that occasion when a deny decision is received in spite of all the efforts by a student to select appropriate colleges. Remember the information you just read about the competition for seats among students entering college in record numbers. You should like all the colleges on your list and want to attend any one of them. It is important to remember that you will have choices. Even with this setback, you need to continue to submit your applications and keep on top of your deadlines. There are other great schools waiting for you to join their freshman class in the fall, but it won't happen if you don't continue to apply.

> While waiting for responses from your colleges, keep in touch with your counselor. Remember that you're not alone, and there are strategies that can be instituted as the responses come in.

ALTERNATIVE PATHS

We have talked about some of the reasons a college may reject an applicant, but no matter what the reason is, disappointment is a natural response. Try to keep things in perspective and work through these feelings in a healthy way. Seek advice and support from the people who have proven they were there for you in the past. Depending on the situation at this point, you might also consider some alternatives.

The Two-Year College

The four-year approach may not be the best option for you, especially if your grades and test scores are weak. Why not try starting at a two-year junior or community college and then transferring after a year or two? You might opt to complete the associate degree in a transfer program that is part of a four-year university. Some two-year schools have special articulation agreements with some very fine colleges that recognize all credits transferred in from the two-year school. This program gives students status as a junior at the university while allowing them the time to mature and strengthen their study skills and academic records.

Or if you want to choose a major like engineering and find that your high school math level is not high enough for entry into four-year engineering programs, the two-year college will allow you the opportunity to gain the background you need while taking courses toward an engineering major.

There's More to College than a "Name"

The other option is to look at the less competitive colleges and universities and not get stuck on a "name." Instead of pouring all your energy into being admitted to that name college, look at those schools that may have less competitive enrollment but provide a sound educational experience. These schools can give you a solid background educationally and an excellent beginning for life.

THE FINAL CUT: HOW DO I DECIDE?

The long wait has ended. The results are in, and you have your acceptances in hand. Even some of your stretch schools are in the acceptance pile. How do you make the final cut?

In some cases you may be very clear by now about the college that is your first choice. If it is in the pile of acceptances, the decision is easy. But what if the choice is not so clear? What if there are several schools in the acceptance pile that look good to you? What can you do to make the decision?

Make your decision carefully. Set a deadline for yourself and stick to it. Something will click, and the decision will be made.

A Return Visit

Visit the campuses again. Returning to a college or university is a good way to get closure. Because this decision is for real, you will go back with a different attitude and a more critical eye this time. How does your area of concentration look to you now? Really delve into the academic offerings at the schools. Check those bulletins and course selection catalogs. Sit in on some classes in your major. Which school has the stronger offering? Will you be happy there for four years?

Check to see how far along the new projects are that the administration said would be ready for next year. I know one student who was told his very expensive liberal arts college intended to build a black box theater the next year. He has since graduated as a theater major from that college, but there is still no black box theater.

Talk to more people while you are there. Listen carefully, but don't become overwhelmed by what you hear. Are there certain things that are essential to you about a school? Is there anything that people are saying that is rubbing you the wrong way? Listen to your feelings.

Some Other Issues That Can Get in the Way

It is important to stay on track when trying to make your decision. It is helpful to talk to others, but do not become distracted by unwanted opinions or someone else's problems. There are periods in the college selection process when you may be the recipient of uninvited information or the target of unsolicited opinions. Decision time can be one of those periods.

Other students will be getting their acceptances, too, and if they are in a competitive mode, they may be broadcasting their results. It has never ceased to amaze me how freely some students will fictionalize their results to avoid the possibility of looking bad to others. Don't believe everything you hear. Don't let your attention be diverted from your own hard-won success at winning a place in college.

In Chapter 3, I talked about the importance of having a heart-to-heart talk with your parents or guardians early on in the college entrance process. If that happened and went well, you should be well-positioned to make a decision that you and your parents are happy with. On the other hand, you may be faced with a difficult situation if you and your parents have different ideas about your college decision. Some parents view their son's or daughter's acceptance to a competitive college as a badge of honor. They consider it a positive reflection on them that is their right to share with the world. Others project a sense of failure and disappointment because their child has not met their expectations. Or parents may be placing inordinate pressure on their child to enroll in a particular college without allowing them the space to make their own decision.

What do I tell students facing parental problems over a college decision? First, I review with them the criteria for their decision. Are the criteria legitimate? I reinforce that college is *their* decision and go over with them the steps they have taken to get to where they are. I offer to role-play with them a conversation with their parents so that they have an opportunity to get their thoughts together before they sit down to actually talk with their parents. Is another visit with the parents to the college of the student's choice a possibility? Could the admissions department of the college help in some manner? The bottom line: If it is about money, it is a hard argument for a student to win. If it is an ultimatum—this college or nothing—the student may not have a choice. Perhaps the family may be able to come to some compromise: a possibility of transfer if the student tries the parents' first choice and really hates it after a year.

There can be a great deal of distraction around you as you attempt to make a decision. It is important to keep your goal in mind. You need to make a decision and respond back to the college of your choice by

May 1, unless you have been given another deadline. Give your decision careful consideration, take the time you need, and involve the people you need. Set a deadline for yourself, if necessary, and stick to it. Something will click, and the decision will be made.

Committing to the College of Your Choice

Now that you have decided, you need to let the colleges know. Complete the required forms and mail them to the college of your choice accepting its offer of admissions. Arrange to complete the other components of your acceptance package. Most colleges require a physical exam and an updated copy of immunizations. You will also have to complete a roommate form, a description of your likes and dislikes, and a dormitory request form. Some colleges will ask you to complete your course selections for the fall, either with this initial packet or shortly afterward. Don't forget to pay your deposit, usually $200 to $250, to secure your place in the fall class. At some point, you will be given a date for freshman orientation and asked for a confirmation.

> Once you have made your choice, don't wait to notify your other choices. Some other student may be waiting for the spot that had your name on it.

What about the other colleges that have sent you acceptances? You will need to send them a polite note declining their offer of admissions and thanking them for their time and efforts in considering your application. Do this as soon as you have made up your mind about your final choice. There may be other students on their waiting list, and a spot for them cannot be opened until you respond. For their sake, complete this task as quickly as possible.

You have made your decision. You are feeling confident about your choice and relieved to have the decision final. What's next? Paying for it, of course.

Paying for College

Let's go back to the car analogy I used in Chapter 4. This time let's concentrate on how you will pay for your car. You have decided on a sporty little economy car, the base model with no special features. It is only $14,000. You are trading in the used car you purchased a year ago because you cannot keep up with the repair bills on it. The dealer offers you $4,000 for your trade-in, and you are negotiating a $10,000 loan at 6.9 percent with a five-year payback period. The monthly payment will be $197.54, and the payback amount at the end of your loan will be $11,852.40. The car depreciates the minute you turn the key and drive it off the lot. Every month you own it, the car is worth less and less.

You will have to take a part-time job to make the car payments. After a while, you may find that you need to increase the hours you work in order to pay the car insurance. Your job may begin to interfere with your studies, and you will have to sit down and reprioritize your life to get everything in balance. Because school has to come first and the job to pay for the car comes second, your social life suffers. Wasn't improving your social life one of the reasons why you bought the car?

YOU'RE IN—NOW, HOW DO YOU PAY FOR IT?

You will take out a loan to buy a car, but you will think twice about taking out a loan to pay for your college education. Why?

The payback for every dollar you spend on your education is an investment in you. Your education is not going to devalue, and no one can take it away from you. It is portable and will travel with you all over the world. That is more than you can say about that sporty little car. In addition, the interest that you pay on your college loan is tax deductible. You cannot say that about a car loan.

The best advice I can give you about pricing colleges is not to look at the sticker price until the very end. You want to save your parents from as much sticker-price shock as you can. There are many ways to pay for college, and after considering all the different types of aid available, in the end, a private college may cost the same or only slightly more than a state university.

How Much Does It Cost to Go to College?

In general, college fees and expenses will vary based on distance from home, type of school (two- or four-year, private or public), and the cost of housing, either in a dorm or in a rental apartment near campus.

Most of the differences are easy to calculate. Attending a college that is an hour's drive away with a friend who has a car or attending a college that is a $300 plane ticket away means not only spending more money each time you come home but coming home less often. Sharing an $800-a-month apartment with three friends will cost less than a $7,000-a-year dorm room—but don't forget to figure in the cost of food for the apartment. Will you use that meal ticket your mother insisted you buy or will you eat frozen pizzas and french fries off paper plates while watching cable in the apartment? By the way, who is paying for the cable?

Figuring out the cost of public versus private schools is not as obvious as it may seem. At first glance, it seems that private colleges are always more expensive than public colleges, so students often shy away from exploring private schools. Yet, there are times after the financial aid package is factored in when a private college can be less expensive for you than a state university. Because their endowments are larger, private schools often offer additional financial resources in the form of grants and scholarships. Once aid is estimated, the cost of a private institution may be only an additional $1,000 to $2,000 per year over the cost of a public education. The offerings at these institutions may outweigh the additional cost to you. Over time, when you consider the financial payback of a college education, that $1,000 or $2,000 per year will be minimal.

Be sure to investigate what financial programs your state may offer for private school tuition reduction or aid. Some states have contracts with private colleges to provide access to fields that are considered in high demand. In Florida, for instance, the Florida Tuition Equalization program pays the balance of private college tuition for students who enter understaffed majors. Iowa, Georgia, and several other states have similar programs. In some cases, these programs can offer significant savings. Keep all your options open, and don't eliminate a private college because you are concerned about financing your education. Your needs and the way you match up with the college should always come first.

To get a clearer picture and to better understand what we are talking about here, let's look at some fees.

Average Annual Costs

(at the end of the 1990s, for full-time undergraduate)

Tuition

- Public community college (two-year, AA-granting) $1,501 (in-state fees)
- Public university (four-year, BA-granting) $3,111 (in-state fees)
- Private college or university (four-year, BA-granting) $13,664

Books and Fees

- Public $590
- Private $600

Room and Board

- Public $4,500
- Private $7,000

Other Expenses

- Travel, entertainment $1,869
- Telephone, personal $1,530

Total Costs

- Public community college $8,460
- Public four-year college $10,070
- Private four-year college $22,794

Federal and other need-based aid can reduce tuition charges substantially. National figures for a recent academic year showed that once all aid was factored in, the total cost for public community colleges was about $1,200 less than the total tuition figure; for public universities, it was about $4,900 less; and for private colleges and universities, it was about $8,700 less.

By the year 2000, more than eighty colleges in the United States had tuition, room, and board tipping the scales at $32,000 a year. That means that a four-year education at these schools is in the $130,000 range. Although only 6 percent of all college students attend institutions with fees in this range, very few students can afford a college education without some kind of financing. The average indebtedness for undergraduates coming out of a four-year institution is $16,500. Even the most energetic and resourceful scholarship hunter may not be able to piece together enough grants, scholarships, and work-study to cover the costs of a four-year education. Most students find that even with exhausting their own savings and tapping their parents', they still need to arrange for government and private loans.

Who Is Getting the Money?

The majority of aid is based on financial need. Middle-class families may feel that they will not be able to qualify for need-based financial aid, but in reality about 30 percent of students with family incomes between $50,000 and $70,000 receive grants that average $1,700 each. At private institutions, almost 80 percent of students receive grants or scholarships, which average $6,000 each. There are also some awards, grants, and scholarships reserved for minority students.

At private institutions, almost 80 percent of students receive grants or scholarships, which average $6,000 each.

The awarding of need-based aid boils down to whether your family's expected contribution (EFC) toward your college education, as calculated by federal formulas, exceeds the cost of the school. If it does, your basis for "official" need vanishes. However, a number of factors are considered in calculating EFC. Your parents' income is only one factor. Their assets, the family's expenses, and family size are all considered when the calculations are made for EFC.

What Are Some of the Ways to Pay for College?

Take a look at the box "The Trilogy of Financial Aid," below. You have three choices: grants and scholarships, work-study, and loans.

Except at the most competitive institutions, there are merit scholarships and non-need-based awards available. If you are in the top half of a college's freshman class, you may be eligible for $500 to $2,000 in scholarship money. All you may need to do is write a brief essay in

---

Trilogy of Financial Aid

There are three ways you can receive financial aid for college:

1. Grants and Scholarships
   This is money that does not have to be repaid after graduation.

2. Work-Study
   This is money you earn through work at your own college or university that is paid directly to the school to help pay for your tuition.

3. Loans
   This is money that you borrow and must repay with interest over time.

---

response to a question on the application. If you have musical or performing arts talent, if you are a writer or a debater, or if you demonstrate other talents, you may be eligible for merit awards presented annually by a wide range of colleges. A word of caution to athletes: keep studying. Athletics are not as big a payoff as you may think. Only about 1 percent of undergraduates are enrolled on athletic scholarships.

Most schools will automatically screen their candidates for merit- and talent-based scholarships. Some schools may require an audition or portfolio in the fine and practical arts categories. Often, the financial aid package offered by colleges to their students is a combination of need- and merit-based aid.

WHAT ARE SOURCES FOR FINANCIAL AID?

Before we look at the sources of financial aid, there are three rules to keep in mind as you do research about, find, apply for, and win financial support.

- Watch Your Deadlines.
  The sources for funding set their own deadlines, and these

In Case You Think Your Circumstances Are Unique:

- Seven out of 10 full-time students receive some form of financial aid.
- Financial aid covers about 40 percent of the budget for full-time students.
- Grants and loans are the most common types of student aid.
- Grants cover 20 percent of the budget for full-time undergraduates.
- More than half of all full-time undergraduates were receiving grant aid by the end of the 1990s.
- One in 5 undergraduates comes from a family with income below $20,000 a year.

---

deadlines differ from source to source. Thousands of dollars are lost to students each year because they let the deadlines slip by. You need to monitor application due dates carefully.

- Never Assume You Won't Qualify.
  Because every college can set need-based levels for financial aid that may differ from the federal guidelines, you may be eligible for college-based support. These college-determined levels vary from one college to another, so even if you are not eligible for support from one college, that does not necessarily mean you will not receive money from another.

- Read Your Award Letters Carefully.
  What is the award letter really saying? Because every college and university delivers its financial aid packages and non-need-based awards differently, it is important to compare the bottom lines after you have received your acceptances. It is not the total amount on the bottom of the form that matters. What matters is how you are getting the money. Financial aid packages where the offer is heavier on the grant side and lighter on the loan side are preferable. If you have several colleges on your list of acceptances that meet all your other criteria, comparing the final cost to you may well be another factor to consider before you make that final cut.

Borrowing as an Option

Borrowing is a viable option to pay for an education that will be invaluable in expanding your life choices. Borrowing responsibly and knowing the cost of different loans up front is important in order to make an intelligent determination. If you did not discuss paying for college in your initial conversation with your parents or guardian, this is the time to do it. You need to talk about how you will pay for college and how much you really need to borrow. Together, you need to find answers to questions such as:

- What are your parents' plans to pay for college?
- What expectations do they have about your contribution to college expenses?
- What are the limits on loans that you and your parents are willing to take on to pay for college?
- What other options are available to you and your family to pay for college?

Every family will answer these questions differently, but it is important to devise a strategy that works for your family. Next, it is important to learn as much as you can about what options are available to you.

Federal Financial Aid Programs

Federal education loan programs offer lower interest rates and more flexible repayment plans than most consumer loans, thus making them an attractive way to finance your education. The federal government currently spends only half of 1 percent of its budget on grants to help low- and middle-income families pay for college. However, federal grant, loan, and work-study programs still account for around 73 percent of all available student aid—$44 billion out of a total $60. 5 billion by the end of the 1990s. Grants from institutions and private sources accounted for another 19 percent ($11.2 billion), and state grants provided the remaining 6 percent ($3.3 billion). Because of the cost of higher education, students increasingly have been forced to finance their education through loans rather than grants or work-study.

The federal government has a number of programs to assist students and their parents with paying for college. Read through the list below and see what you think you may qualify for. But until you complete and submit your Free Application for Federal Student Aid (FAFSA), you won't know. For information on filling out the FAFSA, see page 162.

Name of Program	Type of Program	Maximum Yearly Award
Federal Pell Grant	Need-based grant	$3,125
Federal Supplemental Educational Opportunity Grant (FSEOG)	Need-based grant	$4,000
Federal Work-Study	Need-based part-time job	no maximum
Federal Perkins Loan	Need-based loan	$3,000
Subsidized Stafford Loan (FFEL/ Direct)	Need-based loan	$2,625 (first year)
Unsubsidized Stafford Loan (FFEL/Direct)	Non-need-based loan	$2,625 (first year)
PLUS Loans	Non-need-based parent loan	Up to the cost of education

(Note: Both Direct and FFEL Stafford Loans have higher maximums after the freshman year.)

Federal Subsidized Loan Program

The U.S. Department of Education operates two major student loan programs: the Federal Family Education Loan (FFEL) program and the William D. Ford Direct Loan Program. These are the largest loan programs under the federal higher education assistance umbrella, accounting for 92 percent of federal higher education loans.

The FFEL program provides loans to students at postsecondary institutions through the use of private lenders and guaranty agencies such as banks, credit unions, or savings and loan associations. Students must demonstrate financial need to be eligible for subsidized loans.

The Direct Loan program uses U.S. Treasury funds to provide loan capital directly to participating institutions of higher education, which, in turn, make loans to students. The money does not pass through a private lender. A college must participate in the Direct Loan program in order for students to qualify for a Direct Loan.

Both Direct Loan and FFEL programs make available two kinds of loans: Stafford Loans to students and Plus Loans to parents. The difference between these loans is the lending source, but for the borrower, the difference is virtually invisible. Students may not receive both a Direct Loan and an FFEL for the same period of time, but they may receive both in different enrollment periods.

> In 1976, loans accounted for 20 percent of federal assistance for college. By 1996, students were receiving three quarters of their aid in loans.

- *Subsidized Stafford Loans*
  Subsidized Stafford Loans are made on the basis of demonstrated student need and have their interest paid by the government during the time the student is in school. Loan repayment begins six months after a student's status drops to less than half-time, and the repayment schedule may be stretched to ten years. The interest rate is 0 percent while the student is enrolled in school (the federal government subsidizes this part) and has an 8.5 percent cap during the length of the repayment. Borrowers must pay a 4 percent fee that is deducted from the loan proceeds.

- *Unsubsidized Stafford Loans*
  This loan is not based on need, meaning that students are eligible regardless of family income. The same interest and repayment terms apply as with the Subsidized Stafford Loans. The exception is that the interest accrues during the student's time in school and in the six-month grace period after the student is no longer enrolled full time.

- *PLUS Loans*
  PLUS Loans are loans for parents of dependent students and are designed to help families with cash-flow problems. There is no needs test for which to qualify, and parents may borrow up to the cost of a child's education, minus other financial aid received. Repayment begins sixty days after the money is advanced, and

interest accrues at a rate not to exceed 9 percent. A 4 percent fee is subtracted from the proceeds. Parents generally must have a good credit record to qualify for PLUS Loans. As with Stafford Loans, PLUS Loans may be processed under either the Direct Loan or the FFEL system.

Federal Perkins Loan Program

Perkins loans are coordinated by your college's financial aid office to provide low-interest (5 percent) loans to students with exceptional financial need (students with the lowest Expected Family Contribution). The funds are supplied by Federal Capital Contributions, institutional matching funds, and collections from previous borrowers. Borrowers may take up to ten years to repay the loan, beginning nine months after they graduate, leave school, or drop below half-time status. No interest accrues while they are in school, and under certain circumstances, some or all of these loan amounts may be forgiven for borrowers who work in certain occupations or in certain geographic areas after graduation. Occupations such as nursing, law enforcement, teaching in many rural or urban locations, or serving as VISTA or Peace Corps volunteers may meet the criteria for loan forgiveness.

Pell Grant Program

This program is the largest grant program—almost 4 million students receive Pell Grant awards each year. The grant is intended to be the base or starting point of assistance for lower income families. Pell Grants are awarded to the neediest students; eligibility is determined by Expected Family Contribution. The average family income of Pell Grant recipients who were dependent on their parents for financial support was $19,259. The maximum grant for 1999–2000 was $3,125; this number is expected to increase in coming years.

Supplemental Educational Opportunity Grants (SEOG)

This program, handled through college financial aid offices, helps bridge the gap between the maximum Pell Grant and the cost of a particular college. The college or university supplements the student's Pell Grant. The federal share of a student's award cannot exceed 75 percent of the total, and the remaining 25 percent is contributed by the institution. It is an efficient, cost-effective way to aid students and encourage them to continue with their education. Awards in a recent year ranged from $100 to $4,000, with the average grant being $700. More than 77 percent of students who received federal SEOG grants came from families with annual incomes of less than $20,000; more than 90 percent had family incomes under $30,000.

Leveraging Educational Assistance Partnerships (LEAP)

Formerly known as the State Student Incentive Grant (SSIG) Program, LEAP provides incentive grants to states to help students pay for their postsecondary education. States are required to provide at least 50 percent of the funding for the program. To receive the state grants, students must demonstrate financial need. In a recent year, some 650,000 students received funds through LEAP, with the average amount being $600. The median family income was $12,053.

Federal Work-Study (FWS) Program

This program provides part-time jobs for students who need financial aid for their educational expenses. Students work on an hourly basis in a job on or off campus and are paid at least the federal minimum wage. Federal funds cover up to 75 percent of a student's wages, with the rest being paid by the institution, the employer, or another donor. In a recent year, average earnings were $1,123. Nearly 52 percent of the students who were part of the work-study program came from families with annual incomes of less than $30,000. College financial aid offices supervise this program on campuses.

Specialized Federal Programs

Federal agencies other than the Department of Education offer college assistance. These specialized programs may be need- or merit-based and consist of grants and scholarships, internships, and fellowships. In addition, service programs like Americorps, VISTA, and the Peace Corps offer paid opportunities and deferment or forgiveness of part of a federal student loan.

Federal Financial Aid Eligibility

There are a number of criteria that need to be met to be eligible for federal financial aid programs, including grants, work-study, and loans.

Whether you think you are eligible for federal financial aid or not, it is important that you complete a FAFSA form.

These criteria are evaluated according to a formula that is determined by the federal government every year. The formula requires that you:

- Demonstrate financial need.
- Earn a high school diploma or GED or pass an independently administered test approved by the U.S. Department of Education.
- Be enrolled in an eligible postsecondary program.
- Be a U.S. citizen or an eligible noncitizen.
- Register with the Selective Service if you are a male between the ages of 18 and 25.
- Make satisfactory academic progress, as defined by your school.

Whether you think you are eligible for federal financial aid or not, it is important that you complete a FAFSA form. This is the federal instrument for determining financial need. However, this same form is often used by a school's financial aid office as a basis for calculating need- or merit-based financial aid that is sponsored by other sources that are available through the college or university.

Filling Out the FAFSA

Before sitting down to complete the FAFSA form, you will need to gather the following financial records:

- Your parents' (or guardian's, if that person[s] will be responsible for any of your expenses) income tax return for the last year, estimated if necessary
- Your income tax return for the same period, estimated if necessary
- W-2 forms for your parents (or guardian) and you OR the December 31 pay stubs for you and your parents (or guardian)

A FAFSA form is available from your high school guidance office or career center or through a college's financial aid office. You can also get a copy by calling 800-4-FED-AID (toll-free) or find it on the Web at www.fafsa.ed.gov. Complete the form on line or mail it as quickly after January 2 as possible. Deadlines vary by college and state; some are as early as February 1.

You will need to have your parents complete their income tax calculations for your junior year. They do not have to mail their return to the IRS until April 15, but they need to calculate their taxes for purposes of determining your eligibility for aid. You will need to calculate your income tax return as well because the income you earn is used to determine financial need, too.

> If your employer or your parents' employers do not supply W-2 forms quickly after January 1 (they have until the last day of January), it can make it difficult to complete your income tax calculations accurately. Solution? Save your last pay stub and ask your parents to do the same. The last stub totals the income and tax deductions for the year.

In order to complete the FAFSA form, you will need to know whether you and your parents used the 1040, 1040A, or 1040EZ form to file your tax returns. The FAFSA directs you to the exact lines on these tax forms from which to take the numbers to fill in the FAFSA.

You must place on the form the federal college code (not the code from the SAT/ACT program) for all the colleges to which you have applied. Ask your guidance counselor for the codes or retrieve them from the FAFSA Web site. The result of your eligibility test will be supplied to your colleges electronically by the federal government.

If you need help filling out the forms, see if your guidance department holds a Financial Aid Night. The guidance department will invite a Director of Financial Aid from one of the local colleges to come in and walk you and your parents through filling out the FAFSA. If your school does not offer such a program, ask your guidance counselor for help.

FAFSA Notification

At the same time you receive a response back on a form called a Student Aid Report (SAR) from the government, your results will be sent to your colleges electronically. If you filed electronically, results will be available in two to three weeks. If you filed by paper, it will take four to six weeks for your FAFSA to be processed. If you do not receive the results within this time period, call 319-337-5665. The SAR does not supply you with the real money numbers you need in order to determine your actual assistance, but it will indicate whether you are eligible and will ask you to check that all information is correct. If there are corrections to be made, you are given instructions for returning the corrected information.

Your colleges will interpret your eligibility, and you will receive an award letter from the financial aid office. Each college's award package is determined by the extent of its financial resources. This means that money packages may vary greatly from one college to another. The award document will specify the types of aid you are eligible for and the amount in each category that you will receive from that college. Your financial aid eligibility is the difference between the cost of education and the Expected Family Contribution (EFC). The cost of education includes tuition and fees, room and board, books and supplies, transportation, and miscellaneous expenses. The federal government performs a needs analysis on the financial data you submitted in order to determine your EFC.

> Getting financial aid is a first-come, first-served situation. The sooner you submit the completed FAFSA form, the more likely a college's money will be available to you.

College and University Aid Programs

The information you just read covers the federal financial aid tool—the FAFSA—for calculating financial need. But for those of you who have private colleges and universities on your final list, you may need to complete an additional form, the College Scholarship Service (CSS) Financial Aid Profile.

Because of increasing endowments, careful investing, and very active alumni donation programs, about 400 private colleges and universities are able to sponsor their own need-based and non-need-based aid programs. They have more than $2 billion in scholarships to administer annually, and these awards can amount to nearly 20 percent of all aid to students. These colleges and universities ask students and their families to submit both the FAFSA and an application called a PROFILE.

The College PROFILE Form

While the FAFSA is free and available from your guidance office or through the government's FAFSA Web site, the PROFILE is fee-based. There is a cost attached to each report you want sent to a college on your list that requires the PROFILE. You register either by calling the College Board at 800-788-6888 (toll-free) or by accessing the Board's Web site at www.collegeboard.org. The College Board has an arrangement through its College Scholarship Service with the colleges and universities that use the PROFILE to process PROFILE applications. When you register, you will be asked to furnish some basic information so that the PROFILE package you receive will be customized to your specific needs.

In addition to the information about tax returns and W-2s that you need to complete the FAFSA, you will need the following to complete the PROFILE:

- Interest and dividend statements from bank accounts
- Home mortgage information, if applicable
- Debt information

Depending on when interest and dividend statements, home mortgage data, and loan and credit card statements arrive in January, you and your family may need to do some estimating.

The PROFILE was developed several years ago when the federal government changed the FAFSA form and eliminated home equity, interest and dividend, and debt information from the equation for estimating financial need. Private colleges felt that equity in the family home was an important factor for financing a private college education. In addition, the PROFILE expects a minimum student contribution; FAFSA requires no student contribution. However, the PROFILE allows you to explain special circumstances that may impact your family's finances, such as medical expenses and private secondary school costs. The form also has supplemental questions that help colleges and universities determine eligibility for restricted scholarships and grants, such as scholarships for certain majors or grants for students of certain ethnicities. In general, the EFC calculated through the PROFILE will be higher than what the FAFSA calculates.

For Additional Information on Financial Aid

For more information on how these loan programs are administered through a particular college or to get answers to questions you may have about a financial aid package, your best resource is the financial aid office at the college. Start there with a financial aid counselor. If you have general questions about filing forms or the government's FAFSA program, the following are some numbers and Web sites you may find helpful:

1. Federal Student Aid Information: 800-433-3243 (toll-free) for questions about federal student aid, eligibility, forms, or publications
2. Processing Center for FAFSA: 319-337-5665 to check whether your FAFSA form was processed and to request duplicates
3. Department of Education: www.ed.gov to complete your FAFSA form on line, get additional information on federal student aid, or learn more about the tax credit and savings programs for higher education.
4. For help with FAFSA on line: 800-801-0576 (toll-free) to help you through the online completion process
5. State Supported Assistance Programs and Agencies: www.ed.gov/offices/OPE/agencies. html
6. Peterson's Financial Aid Information: www.petersons.com to help you with calculating your EFC and as a resource for scholarships and information about financial aid
7. The College Board Web site: www.collegeboard.org

Steps in the PROFILE Process

The process for completing the PROFILE is similar to what you did for the FAFSA.

- Register on line or by phone to get your customized PROFILE application.
- Gather all the information you need to complete the PROFILE on paper or on line.
- Obtain the codes from the back of the PROFILE booklet or the Web site for each of the colleges and scholarship programs that are requesting the PROFILE.
- Complete the form either on paper or on line.

- If you use the paper form, mail it and your check to the address listed on the PROFILE for the College Board. If you fill out the form on line, you will need a secure browser and a valid credit card.
- When you receive your CSS acknowledgement form, you will need to check the information for accuracy, make corrections as needed, and return the corrected form to CSS.

Other Ways to Help Pay for College

There are several other options for paying for your college education that you should think about. Some relate to tax benefits, one to service in the military, and the others are a mix of private-sector initiatives.

The Military Option

Check the Web for information on programs offered by different branches of the armed services.

- Army
  www.goarmy.com
- Navy
  www.navy.mil
- Marine Corps
  www.usmc.mil
- Airforce
  www.af.mil
- Coast Gaurd
  www.uscg.mil
- National Guard
  www.ngb.dtic.mil

The Army, Navy, Marine Corps, Air Force, Coast Guard, and National Guard are all looking for a few good men and women—and they are willing to pay. If you are already considering the military after graduation or have not really thought about it, this may be the time to take a good look. For example, enlistment could help you repay your government-insured and other approved loans. One third of the loan will be repaid for each year of active duty. Each branch of the military also offers its own educational incentives. Check with a local recruiting office or on the Web for specifics of that service's programs. There are also some general service programs to consider.

The G.I. Bill

Technically known as the Montgomery G. I. Bill, its benefits are available to all enlistees in all branches of the service. The G. I. bill pays up to $14,998 toward education costs at any accredited two-or four-year college or vocational school. The benefit is available either during active duty or up to ten years after discharge. For active duty service, $1,200 of a person's pay ($100 a month for twelve months) is allocated to the person's education fund. The military then contributes up to $14,998. For a reservist, the benefit is only $7,124.

Once enrolled in the G. I. bill program, qualified candidates in the army, navy, or marines can earn an additional $15,425 in education assistance, for a total of $30,000 after discharge.

Reserve Officers' Training Corps (ROTC)

The ROTC offers college scholarships that pay most of the recipient's tuition and other expenses and includes a monthly stipend of $150. The Army, for example, provides an ROTC scholarship of up to $48,000, depending on the tuition of the school, plus a living allowance of $150 a month during the academic year. After graduation, most trainees enter the service as officers and complete a four-year tour of duty. The deadline is December 1 of your senior year. Ask your guidance counselor for help in finding out the details.

Tuition Assistance

All branches of the military pay up to 75 percent of tuition for full-time, active-duty enlistees who take courses at community colleges or by correspondence during their tours of duty. The specifics vary by service. If you are interested, contact each branch of the service.

The Community College of the Air Force

Members of the Air Force, Air National Guard, or Air Force Reserves can convert their technical training or military experience into academic credit, earning an associate degree, an occupational instructor's certificate, or trade school certificate. Participants receive an official transcript for this fully accredited program. Besides enhancing your job opportunities after your tour of duty, you may be able to transfer these credits to a four-year college. College admissions offices would be able to help you determine the possibilities.

Education Tax Benefits for Students and Their Families

Beginning in 1998, tuition tax credits allow families to reduce their tax bill by the amount of out-of-pocket college tuition expenses they pay.

These tax credits are dollar-for-dollar reductions in taxes paid. There are two programs: the HOPE Scholarship Tax Credit and the Lifetime Learning Tax Credit.

- *HOPE Scholarship*

  The Hope Scholarship tax credit helps offset some of the expense for the first two years of college or vocational school. Students or the parents of dependent students can claim an annual income tax credit of up to $1,500—100 percent credit for the first $1,000 of tuition and 50 percent credit on the second $1,000. The credit can be claimed for two years for students who are in their first two years of college and who are enrolled on at least a half-time basis. The credit phases out for joint filers with an income over $100,000 or for single filers with an income over $50,000.

- *Lifetime Learning Tax Credit*

  The Lifetime Learning Tax Credit is the counterpart of the HOPE Scholarship for college juniors, seniors, and graduate students. Parents can claim an annual income tax credit up to $1,000—20 percent of the first $5,000 of tuition (after 2002, this limit will be $2,000). The credit is phased out at the same income levels as the HOPE Scholarship.

- *The Student Loan Interest Deduction*

  The Student Loan Interest Deduction lets borrowers deduct interest paid in the first 60 months (that's five years) of a loan that is used to pay for college. The maximum deduction each taxpayer is permitted to take was $2,000 in 2000 and will increase to $2,500 in 2001 and thereafter. For information, contact the Internal Revenue Service or check its Web site at www.irs.ustreas.gov/prod/hot/not97-605.html.

Check These Possibilities, Too

There are other federal programs and tax benefits, state programs, and employer programs that you should investigate. Leave no possibility unresearched. Some of the programs will help you offset costs while you are in college and some will help you when you have graduated and are trying to balance making a life for yourself with repaying that college loan.

Community service loan forgiveness is available in some areas for students who enter certain careers and work in communities that are designated as understaffed.

- The Exclusion for Employee Education Benefits, also known as the Cafeteria Plans, is an option offered by some employers. This program allows employers to set up a system to make payroll deductions for employees of up to $5,250 a year for undergraduate tuition. The money is tax-free, that is, the employee does not pay income tax on it. Ask your parents to check with the Human Resources or Employee Benefits Departments at work to see if their employers participate.
- In 1998, changes were made to the tax law regarding Individual Retirement Accounts (IRAs) to allow parents and grandparents to set aside designated education IRA accounts that allow for the withdrawal of funds without penalty. If your parents or grandparents are interested, they should check with their banks.
- Some employers offer employer matching funds programs. They match funds for children of their employees who receive scholarships or non-need-based merit grants. Several companies offer scholarship programs to their employee's children. Have your parents investigate these possibilities with their Human Resources or Employee Benefits departments.
- Community service loan forgiveness is available in some areas for students who enter certain careers and work in communities that are designated as understaffed. Some of these jobs are in not-for-profit agencies, in tax-exempt charitable or educational institutions, or in careers such as nursing and teaching. Check with your financial aid or guidance office to find out whether the state sponsors these programs and where you can learn more about them.

AVOIDING SCHOLARSHIP SCAMS

Now that you have identified some of the legitimate sources for financial aid assistance, let's talk about some you need to avoid.

Consider this scenario. Your parents receive a letter in the mail inviting them to a hotel conference room for a financial aid seminar. Some of your parents' friends with children in high school also receive the letter, and all the parents decide to attend because financing their children's college education is a big concern for them. You get to the seminar along with some 500 other parents and their teenage children. Subtle wording on the posters and PowerPoint presentation suggest that the sponsor is some official organization, maybe even a government information group. The professional-looking brochures that are handed out are filled with promises to "get you at least $500 in scholarships or financial aid or your money back!" You'll get help to fill out that horrible, complicated FAFSA form, too!

A well-dressed and well-rehearsed salesman talks about how much money is wasted because "people just don't know how to tap into it." He's going to tell you how—for a price. The price will range from $500 (that financial aid package they are guaranteeing) to $1,200. He wants your bank account number or credit card payment on the spot or you will be given the opportunity to sign an agreement to have your paycheck garnished every week to pay the fee.

What is the reality? You will get very little help. What you get is a computer-generated booklet. None of the information is personalized, and you might as well burn the list of colleges they send you if you bought the DELUXE package. This is the college scholarship scam, and it is big business—as big as the list of college-bound students each year.

Here's How a Scholarship Scam Works

Many great things in life are free, but a college education is not one of them. If it sounds too good to be true, it probably is. There are legitimate organizations that can help you find scholarship money, but if any of the following statements apply to the organization you are considering using, chances are you're in for a scam.

1. The companies are always "out-of-state" with official sounding names.
2. You are guaranteed a scholarship or your money back, but just try to find them after the seminar or after you read the small print. The best lawyer in town couldn't get your money back.
3. The company claims to have secrets about obtaining financial aid information that no one else has.

> To report a scholarship scam, fill out the Federal Trade Commission's fraud complaint form on line at www.ftc.gov, or call 877-382-4357 (toll-free).

4. Federal aid programs are a bureaucratic nightmare. The company will do all the work for you.
5. The company offers to do a scholarship search for a small additional fee.
6. The sales pitch may include, "Did you know that you have been selected by a national foundation or you are a finalist in a contest?" The problem is you never entered the contest.
7. The salespeople practice the hard sell. They are very pushy and try to get you to commit that night.

These companies prey on the misinformed and often the neediest people. They are found more and more often on the Web and can be very clever about the way they draw you into their sites. Look out for scholarship matching services, and check their fees up front.

Where Can You Go for Help?

The financial aid process is a complicated one, and everyone could use some sound advice on trying to navigate it. There are good scholarship services out there, but experience has told me that many of the scholarships available come in small amounts, $250 to $500, and are sponsored by local organizations. It involves some work to find them, which is the subject of the rest of this chapter. Where can you look for help sorting out the tangle of financial aid? First, check with your guidance department, and be sure to attend the financial aid night if your school offers one. Take your FAFSA with you.

Depending on your resources, you might hire a professional student financial aid adviser who is a member of the National Association of Student Financial Aid Administrators (NASFAA). These individuals have often been financial aid officers at major universities and are very familiar with the nuances of financial aid programs. There are also members of the National Association of College Admissions Counselors (NACAC) who are private counselors and coach students and families on the ins and outs of the college process and financial aid programs.

You can also try your own scholarship search on the Web. Remember, though, that the bulk of financial aid that students receive

> Accountants are good sources for information about recent changes in the educational tax laws and for help with completing the FAFSA and the PROFILE.

comes from the federal government or from the colleges and universities to which they apply. In order to be eligible for these monies, you have to complete the FAFSA form and possibly the PROFILE as the first step.

CREATING YOUR OWN SCHOLARSHIP SEARCH

Don't believe everything you hear about "scholarship money drying up." That has not been my experience or the experience of my students. They secured more than $2.8 million in scholarships last year, with 50 percent of the class of 422 receiving at least one scholarship each. I publish a 60-page scholarship list every three weeks and have no problem filling the pages with a wide range of scholarship offerings. Why am I mentioning this? To tell you that if you look hard enough for scholarship money, you will be able to find it.

Where Does the Money Come From?

As you begin your search, you will find that there are a variety of sources for scholarship money. Begin by looking close to home. There are small local businesses whose owners are graduates of your high school and still have fond memories of their days at the school. In an effort to repay the help they received from the school, they give scholarships to deserving students. Local business owners may also offer scholarships to local colleges or to students in particular fields of concentration.

There are national and multinational corporations with factories, offices, or stores in your community that believe that investing in the nation's youth through scholarships to colleges and vocational/technical schools will earn them a good return on their investment. They understand that you are the workforce of tomorrow, and that for them to compete, they will need an educated workforce. If these corporations want to assist with your education, why not let them?

Many local, state, and national service and professional organizations and associations as well as civic groups and foundations consider education as part of their mission and devote many hours to fundraising

Game Plan for Getting into College

to further it. The dollars they raise are counted in the millions, and the scholarships are offered in the hundreds of thousands. If you meet their criteria, they want to assist your efforts to obtain a college education. They feel that by supporting you, they are supporting their mission.

As I discussed earlier, colleges and universities also sponsor their own need- and merit-based scholarship awards to entice students to their campuses. These awards run the gamut from academics to the arts to athletics.

Where to Start Your Scholarship Search

How do you find these sources and secure scholarship money? Check with your guidance office to see what scholarship assistance it offers. Does the department publish a monthly listing of scholarships? Are local scholarships included? Is there a central bulletin board posting of scholarships that changes each month? Find out what system the department uses to notify students about scholarships, and track it. The sooner you begin, the better.

In addition to postings, your guidance department or career center will have print and electronic resource materials about scholarships. Books on scholarships include a wide range of information that is categorized by major, gender, ethnicity, state, college or university, athletics, extracurricular involvement, and organizations There are even some categories as far-out as left-handed males. It will take you some time to go through the listings, so start early.

Another source of information is scholarship software packages that many guidance departments have. One is the College Board's "Fund Finder" on their EXPAN ScholarshipSearch software. This package reviews your information on financial aid, calculates your family's EFC, and lists more than 3,300 sources for scholarship and financial assistance. EXPAN even lets you create a generic letter requesting that the applications be mailed to you. You print out the letters, mail them off, and wait for the applications to come back.

Or you may find Guidance Informational Services (GIS) software in your guidance department. This package contains a financial aid and scholarship databank that allows you to input your personal information as a profile and request the types of scholarships and financial

> Although most scholarships are for graduating seniors, there are some available for students in grades 9 through 11. If you are in ninth grade, you have four years to bank scholarship money for college. It adds up.

sources that would be most useful for you to investigate. The program then generates a list of hundreds of scholarships. You double-click on each listing, read the criteria, and print those scholarships that meet your needs. Send off your letters requesting applications, complete them when they come, and see what happens.

And Then There Is the Internet

I mentioned earlier about scholarship scams on the Internet, but the Web is a treasure trove of legitimate scholarship resources, too. Its ability to merge your needs with the enormous amount of information in cyberspace can seem like both a blessing and a curse to a graduating senior. With all that you are juggling—school, testing, completing applications, touring campuses and interviewing, along with family responsibilities and your part-time job—you can use all the help you can get. If you know where to look and how to look carefully, the Internet can be the answer to your prayers.

Spinning the Web

The best resources are supplied by the college information people like Peterson's and the College Board. Because they view the financial aid and scholarship search aspects as part of the whole college exploration process, it is not a surprise that they have placed enormous resources into developing outstanding sites.

Peterson's CollegeQuest at www.petersons.com contains a searchable scholarship databank of more than 800,000 different awards for over $2.5 billion in private aid. Using the same format as its *Scholarships, Grants & Prizes* book, the Peterson's site combines speed and vast resources. You will be able to match your interests, talents, and academic ability with specific grant and scholarship programs. The site provides contact information for each award as well as its eligibility and application requirements, deadline, and dollar amount.

The College Board has its Fund Finder on line at collegeboard.org. An online version of the software available in high school guidance offices, Fund Finder lets you search thousands of sources for financial aid and helps you calculate your family's EFC. Fill in your profile and off you go on your search.

> You can try searching for scholarships on search engines like Yahoo and Excite by typing in "scholarships." Read the small print carefully on whatever comes up, and keep in mind that if a site wants money from you, end the connection.

Both of these sites are updated periodically, an important factor when researching scholarships via the Web. You will find as you begin to explore the Web for scholarship resources just how outdated some of this information can be. Some sites are not tidy about maintaining their databases or checking for accuracy.

Ethnic and Minority Scholarship Sites

If you think you may qualify for a scholarship program for a specific ethnic group, check Minority On-line Information Service (MOLIS) at www.sciencewise.com/molis/. This site offers scholarships linked to historically black colleges and universities as well as to scholarships aimed at Hispanic students. The Hispanic Educational Foundation (HEF) offers state and local scholarship listings for students of Hispanic ethnicity. You can find a link to HEF as well as information on dozens of scholarship and financial aid programs of interest to Hispanic students at www.latinolink.com

Sites for Lending Institutions

Sallie Mae's Online Scholarship Service at www.cashe.com/runsearch. html is a good resource for exploring financial aid information. Sallie Mae, which stands for Student Loan Marketing Association (SLMA), is the nation's largest commercial lender resource. It uses the CASHE scholarship database and offers financial aid calculators to assist parents with calculating their EFC.

A number of major lenders like Citibank (www.citibank.com), Wells Fargo (www.wellsfargo.com), and First Union (www.firstunion.com) also offer online financial aid information and application forms for completion on line.

General Resource Sites

There are several other sites that might provide useful information.

Free information on over $1 billion worth of scholarship awards is claimed to be available at www.fastweb.com. You can enter the site, complete the profile, and create your own e-mail box. FastWeb will send scholarships that fit your profile into your e-mail automatically. If you want to apply for one, click and send out the application electronically.

FinAid, the Financial Aid Information Page at www.finaid.org, has a great deal of information about the different types of financial aid and provides links to other relevant sites as well. It provides a good overview of the financial aid situation. In addition, the site offers several calculators that enable you to estimate many useful figures, including projected costs of attendance, loan payments, the amount you will be expected to contribute to your education, and living expenses if you are applying for need-based aid.

It may not be possible for you to research all these sites on the Web. Choose one or two that seem to meet your needs, and let your fingers fly! There's enough here to keep you busy for a while and hopefully help pay for your college experience.

Once You Have the Information

You will find that as the sources and amounts of scholarships vary, so do the applications that you will have to fill out to compete for them. Some organizations have their own applications, and some forms, especially for the larger amounts of money, can be quite extensive. Some will require that you write an essay. Look at it as an opportunity to practice your writing style and refine your "writing-in-your-own-voice" technique.

Even though it can be a great deal of work, piecing together resources to pay for your college education is definitely worthwhile. Free money can go a long way to help you order that extra pizza or phone home just to see what is going on. You will also be thankful you did this once you have graduated and your student loan repayments are smaller than your roommate's, who could not be bothered stitching together a crazy quilt of awards.

What's a Retention Rate?

Chapter 7

"December 23 and winter break is right around the corner," you think as you sit taking notes in your senior American Government class. You are nearly halfway there. Every senior in the country is counting the days until graduation. Some schools even have the days until graduation posted as a tear-off calendar in the cafeteria. If you are on top of the college admissions process, you have taken all your standardized tests, your college applications are in the works, your recommendations are being written, your essay has been revised and polished to near perfection, and your FAFSA form is just waiting for the end-of-year financial information.

"Is it time for senior slump yet?" you ask. The words echo through the hallways from senior classes past. The problem is you cannot figure out what senior slump is. It is something about being able to breeze your way through senior year, riding on your reputation. When does it happen, this senior slump? Maybe it will happen when the acceptances from colleges are in your pocket, and the first semester is behind you, you think. It will be all downhill until graduation—no books, no homework! After all, you will be a second-semester senior!

A word or two of reality is needed here. Senior year courses are a culmination of your academic growth and accomplishments. Logically, the senior schedule should be the toughest of your high school career, and these classes do count. Colleges and universities view them as similar to the courses offered on their campuses. Colleges request that midyear senior transcripts be sent to them so they can monitor the progress of their prospective candidates. These records impact on admissions decisions, especially for those candidates who may be borderline and need a little extra proof to convince the admissions committee of their capacity to handle the academics. Remember, too, that the grades you get on the AP exams in May can earn you college credit and may determine your placement in courses in the fall. As you look at the rest of the year from your seat in that government class, know that there is no time in your future for a senior slump!

SINK OR SWIM: THE FACTS OF FRESHMAN LIFE

Take another look at the title of this chapter. The retention rate is the percentage that a college or university quotes to indicate the number of students who succeed during their freshman year and return to campus in the fall as sophomores. It is an important concept to look at and a question you should ask each and every one of the schools on your list. Why is it important? The retention rate reflects how much support a college or university gives its freshmen and how prepared the students are when they arrive on campus.

Statistically, it has been proven that students who back off their schedules in senior year and lose momentum have a tough time gearing back up to handle the expectations that are placed on them as freshmen in college. Let's think about this statement for a minute. The reading and research requirements in college are far more intense than they are in high school. College requires 3 hours of study for every hour a student sits in the lecture hall, and the responsibility to schedule that study time is placed on the student.

The Freshman Workload

Let's say you manage to sign up early for your courses and get exactly what you want. You have the perfect schedule. Not one of your classes starts before 11 a.m. Your World History class is on Mondays and Wednesdays from 11 to 12:30. Then you break for lunch, which is a good thing since you expect to roll out of bed and skip breakfast to get to class. You then walk leisurely across campus for your Calculus class that begins at 3 and ends at 5. English and Spanish are on Tuesdays and Thursdays from 11 to 3—no time for a lunch break since you have to run from one end of campus to the other, but, hey, you can always eat a granola bar on the way. One class is left, Art Appreciation. It is a little bit of a run to the Fine Arts Building, but you manage to make it by

3:30. You will be finished with your classes and ready for dinner by 6 p.m. The best thing about your schedule? No classes on Fridays.

Not bad, you think, because as a high school student you are spending 7 hours a day, five days a week in class. You can handle a college schedule. But multiply those freshman class hours by three, because for every hour you spend in class, you will need to spend 3 hours studying. What is the total amount of time you will need to devote to your studies in college? If you're attending full-time, you can count on about 60 hours a week in class or studying.

This is how the course load works. You will go to your World History class on the first Monday of the semester and sit there for two hours listening, answering questions, and taking notes. Then you will go right out and buy the books for the course, a 900-page textbook and three supplemental course packets. You are in a rush to buy the books because you already have three chapters to read by Wednesday's class and a three-page paper to write summarizing the reading.

Off to your calculus class. The professor can really make math exciting! But you are back at the bookstore after class to buy the book so you can get started on the four chapters and three problem sets you have to get through before Wednesday. And so on! (By the way, buy all your books at once and before classes begin because you will need the time to study.)

How successful do you think you will be at keeping up with this workload if you go on an extended vacation in your senior year? It is hard to get back into the swing of things if you have been in a senior slump.

> Each class you take means three times as many hours on your own reading and doing research.

The Impact on Your Retention Rate

College dropout rates are high, and each number represents a real person—a student probably much like you, a little apprehensive but excited, too, and filled with expectations for a wonderful, successful four years. What happened? Why don't students return after the first semester or the first year?

The answer is choices. The choices students make determine whether they become a dropout statistic or are calculated by their college in its retention rate. Some of the choices that students will make involve managing academic scheduling and workloads, others will involve socialization, and still others will revolve around adjustment and transition to a new setting. Whatever the issue and the reasons affecting your decisions, the choices you make will determine whether you stay or leave.

How can you tip the balance so the outcome is that happy, successful, productive four years you envision now? Just as there are steps in the college exploration process, there are steps you can take to get the most out of your college career.

IS THERE AN ACADEMIC ADVISER IN THE HOUSE?

The choices students make determine whether they become a dropout statistic or have a successful college experience.

Remember that thick envelope I spoke about in the first chapter? Besides that coveted acceptance letter, it may include financial aid information and forms, a dorm request form, and a questionnaire about your living habits so that the college can attempt to pair you with a compatible roommate. The packet may also contain the college's or university's course selection book, which is the size of a small paperback novel, and a worksheet requesting that you select your courses for your first semester. Included are some instructions that may read something like this:

- Choose courses that meet your core requirements.
- If you have received advanced credit as a result of Advanced Placement exams or challenge testing, you may look at more advanced-level courses. In that case, choose courses starting with a 200 preceding the course identification number in these subject areas.
- Read the prerequisites for the courses you are choosing, and make sure that you have completed these requirements before making your selection.
- Choose five first-choice courses.
- Make a list of two back-up courses for each course you place as your first choice.
- And on and on and on . . . .

You may have stopped after the first statement and are asking yourself, "What's a core requirement?" But don't panic—there is an academic adviser in the house.

Your Academic Adviser

Most of the time, those worksheets schools send out with their acceptance letters are simply meant to get you to review the course selection book and familiarize yourself with the options available to you. This familiarity facilitates the course selection process when you really do sit down to complete your formal request form. This will probably happen during the freshman orientation that you will be invited to attend before school opens. That is when you will meet your academic adviser.

As a freshman, your academic adviser will probably be a senior faculty member, but probably not from your major since many freshmen are still undecided about one. This is your temporary adviser, although temporary may last until you declare a major at the end of your sophomore year. Depending on the size of the school, you may meet with your adviser in his or her office for a counseling session before you make your course selections. In a larger university, you may find yourself seated in a group setting where general information about course requirements and the selection process will be explained. Some schools are swamped with so many students that the course selection process is accomplished via computer and telephone conversations. You may never see a human being.

Once you declare a major, you will be assigned a professor in that department as your adviser. This generally creates a personalized approach to the course selection process and will give you someone you can count on for advice and direction. Tap into this resource and establish a working relationship with your adviser. Advisers can be a wealth of information and help. They will often steer students to graduate programs or to jobs and provide recommendations and contacts after graduation.

A word of advice about the course selection process seems in order here. When you choose the courses you want for a semester, it is also important to look to the future and see where you are going. Setting out course requirements with your adviser for future semesters is a good idea. Besides giving you a sense of direction and the assurance that you are working toward enough credits to graduate, this allows you a fallback position in case you go to sign up and find your first, second, and even third choices have been filled.

Other Sources of Advisement

So far, it may seem as though you may not get much personal attention in making some really big choices as a freshman, but there are some things you can do to help yourself. Remember, I said that college places a great deal of responsibility for your education on you.

First, look for the Resident Adviser who may be assigned to and living in your dorm. These individuals have been put in place to act as a resource for the students living in the dorm, and academic advisement is usually one of their strong points. They are available during odd hours, although they need a good night's sleep once in a while, too. Seek them out, and follow their advice about course requirements and course descriptions.

Then, there is always "ask the kid next door." Not always the best way to do things, but if he or she is studying in your major, your neighbor might be a good resource. Just keep in mind that everyone has personal likes and dislikes. Try to get as much objective, factual information as possible about a professor's teaching style, course syllabus, use of a TA, assignments, and tests. Then make your own decision. The way this professor conducts his or her course may match your personal learning style well.

The newest source for checking out courses is on line. Most dorms today are fully wired, as are computers in the college's library. At many schools, the course selection book is available on line. Check for the name of the professor teaching the course, and then check the course as it was last delivered. You will often find on line the syllabus and reading requirements for the course, the time line for assignments, and, in some cases, even access to communications students have had with the professor regarding questions and concerns. This will let you determine for yourself whether the content is to your liking and if you find the approach to the subject stimulating. You will get a good view of

> Some students change their minds about their majors two and three times before they declare their major in their sophomore year. If you find yourself changing your mind, be sure to revisit your options regularly to make sure you are on target for graduation.

the workload expectations for the course, too. If nothing else, you will have some questions to ask your adviser regarding courses you are considering before you sign up for classes.

SAFETY, DRINKING, AND DRUG ISSUES ON CAMPUS

As one of my returning students once said to a group of seniors during a Senior Transition Day program, "Since you live at college 24 hours a day, a lot of learning goes on outside of the classroom." The college campus is a reflection of society—the same values and issues that are operating in the "real world" are represented in the daily life of a college campus.

Campus Security

Colleges feel strongly about the safety of their students and, as a result, many campuses have instituted several levels of prevention and systems of intervention for campus security. The physical measures that have been put in place on most campuses include electronic entry-card systems, escort services, telephones that are well marked and accessible throughout the campus, adequate illumination, and frequent patrols by security staff members.

The educational programs that have become part of many freshmen orientations are among the most effective intervention methods. A typical program will have the Department of Student Affairs conduct several consciousness-raising sessions to create an awareness of the issue of safety on campus. These programs are presented during large group presentations. But then staff members take their message into the dorms. Late-night dorm talks about coed relations and crime and safety information lend legitimacy to their presentations. Because many of these staff members are also the ones who do counseling intervention when something does go wrong on campus, they are very motivated to get their message across—loud and clear.

Drinking and Drugs

What about drinking and drugs? As I said above, college is a reflection of society. Unfortunately, you probably know some students now who do drugs and alcohol. When you get to college, you will have to make the same kinds of decisions you made at some point in high school about where you stand. The difference is that you will be in a new environment meeting everyone for the first time—and living with them.

In high school, people knew what your comfort level was with drinking and drugs and accepted your decision. You were who you were, and that was it. You had a group of friends who felt as you did, and after a while the issue of drinking or drugs just did not come up. In college you will have to establish your boundaries all over again.

Well, life is all about choices—other people's choices and yours. It will take some energy and thought, conversation, and reflection to establish your comfort zone at college. You will be able to work it out, though, especially if your values are clear and you have your priorities straight. Be prepared, however, that these adjustments will demand your attention and place a strain on your energy. No wonder you are tired so much of the time.

Colleges and universities have realized the extent to which "drinking and drugging the weekend away" has become a problem to the students who do it and to their classmates who have to put up with the aftermath. Schools have begun to make major changes in their attitude and regulation of student drinking. Fraternities are not so welcome on campus as they used to be. Rushing has dropped off on some campuses, and on others administrations have suspended and even closed down some Greek houses. Bars have been restricted to seniors only and in many cases replaced by coffeehouses. Substance-free dorms are available on most campuses, and colleges pay more attention to the social events on their campuses. And remember: Drugs are against the law. If you are caught with a controlled substance on campus, you can be suspended, expelled, or turned over to the law for prosecution.

What have been the results of these changes? There are still places to go to drink, and there always will be, if that is the choice you want to make. But now colleges and universities are making special efforts to provide other interesting and fun options to choose from. The choice is yours.

WHERE DO I GO WITH AN EMOTIONAL OR HEALTH CONCERN?

Freshman year in college can be stressful. You are looking at this sentence and thinking, "What does she think the last two years of high school have been?" Yes, for some—perhaps many—of you, they have been very stressful years, but there were familiar things around you to help ground and support you: your best friend, your parents, your pet, even your annoying younger sibling.

Using Support Services

Your support system has been in place for you for a long time. Friends and family have a history with you, and their patterns of support are well established. They recognize when you need help and know how to offer it in ways that have been proven to work over time. When you go to college, this support will not evaporate, but it may well be a telephone call away—and it just is not the same. Your family and old friends may not know the people you are dealing with, and as each day goes by, the distance that separates you and your old support network from shared experiences becomes emotional as well as physical. You try to explain the events and characters in your new life, but the old network is not there to see for themselves. In addition, your friends from high school are trying to make their own adjustments to their new lives and have their own problems and issues with which to deal.

> You're smart enough to know when you need help, but where do you go on campus to get it?

"I'm a strong person. I can handle this," you might be thinking about now. That's very true. You survived your junior year, didn't you? But as John Donne wrote, "No man (or woman for that matter) is an island unto himself."

Let me relate something that happened to me that brings home the point about asking for help.

I was doing college visits in New England one year. The one place I always visit is the Student Center. These trips start early in the morning, and I need my coffee. The next important place is the ladies room. I go there for the obvious reason, but I also go there to read the notices on the walls and the graffiti on the doors. So I am reading the back of the bathroom stall at one school, and it is just covered in different handwriting and various shades of ink with referral resources at that university for eating disorders. Many women have given brief overviews of their personal experiences and the resources on the campus they have tried. They have included evaluations of the services and descriptions of the style and approaches each therapist uses. Other women have commented on these by writing their own reactions in the margins.

I was a registered nurse before I became a guidance counselor, and nurses, like seniors, think they have seen it all. But those comments caught me off guard. I thought to myself, do the administration and student services at this school recognize what a problem eating disorders are on their campus? Don't they ever paint these doors? Don't they know that visitors to their campus will see this and become concerned? Then I thought, maybe that's less important to them than getting their students the help they need. Even though this was a strange way to advertise campus services, it obviously got the attention of these young women.

That experience raised my awareness about the stress levels on college campuses, how students manifest their stress, and how institutions address these concerns. Since then, I have made it a point when I visit campuses to seek out the student support services centers and health clinics and thoroughly investigate the quality of the care and delivery systems in place. The questions I ask include: How do students access services? How are they informed of the existence of preventative and treatment programs? What outreach programs are offered? What are they like? How do students pay for services?

You need to ask these questions, too—and you need to use the services available to you. Whether you have a bad case of the flu, your roommate's making you crazy, or the stress level is wearing you down, make sure you know what's out there and where to find help when you need it.

LOOKING BACK AND LOOKING AHEAD

A college degree is a special accomplishment. It is a tribute to your perseverance, academic interests, and abilities. It is your next life goal. But before you start moving toward it, take a few minutes to look back and to look around you.

Stop and consider for a moment the people in your life who have been there for you at every juncture. Sometimes we think they must know how we feel about them. Didn't we used to tell them how we felt when we were kids? But have you told them lately? There are special times that mark the passage from one stage of life into the next. Graduation from high school is one of these times. You will be acknowledged—by your graduation ceremony, cards, and gifts-but what about the people you need to acknowledge? Think about devising a way to demonstrate your appreciation in some tangible, permanent way. It will have great meaning to the person to whom you give it.

It has always been a profound experience when I have moved from one place to another and had to pack up my things. It is amazing what treasures I find when I move. I review my life, discarding those things that are only clutter and holding on to those that have meaning for me. Several years ago, I moved and packed up my guidance office and my home. Fifteen years of stuff accumulated at one school was contained in that office. As I went through my desk and file cabinets, I was touched by the notes and mementos from the students, parents, and faculty and staff members who shared themselves with me. I could hold on to those pieces of paper and conjure up the writers as though they were there in my office with me. I thought about who they had been and who they are now. I took every one of those pieces of paper with me.

What do you want to carry with you as you go on your way? College is a place to think about new beginnings. It is a place to try out different things, including different lifestyles. This might be especially true if you come from a small community where you have been locked into one persona all your life. Do you want to abandon the football hero role or the techie image or the grind? Stretching your wings a little and finding new experiences are part of what college is all about. It is a time for change and growth.

Good luck in your college experience!

> What will you bring with you, inside you, that essential piece that makes you who you are?

academic adviser—This is a senior faculty member in your area of concentration who is assigned to advise you on course selections and requirements. Before you declare your major, you will be assigned a temporary faculty adviser.

accelerated study—This program allows you to graduate in less time than is usually required. For instance, by taking summer terms and extra courses during the academic year, you could finish a bachelor's degree in three years instead of four.

admissions decisions

- **admit**—You're in! You are being offered admission to the college to which you applied. Your high school will receive notification, too.
- **admit/deny**—You have been admitted but denied any financial aid. It is up to you to figure out how you are going to pay for school.
- **deny**—You are not in. The decision is made by the college or university admissions committee and is forwarded to you and your high school.
- **wait list**—You are not in yet but have been placed on a waiting list in case an opening becomes available. Schools rank their wait lists in order of priority, and, unfortunately, the more competitive schools have years when they never draw from their wait lists. After a certain time, a rejection notice is sent.

Advanced Placement (AP) courses—High-level, quality courses in any of twenty subjects. The program is administered through the College Board to offer high school course descriptions equated to college courses and correlated to AP examinations in those subjects. High schools provide the courses as part of their curriculum to eligible students. Based on the composite score on an AP test, which ranges from 0 to 5, a college may award college credit or advanced placement to a participating student. A score of a 4 or 5 on the AP test is usually required by colleges for credit or advanced placement in college courses. A 3 is sometimes acceptable in foreign languages and some other subject areas. Some colleges limit the number of AP credits that they will recognize. Check schools' policies on AP credits.

alternative assessment—This method personalizes the admissions process and offers students an opportunity to be viewed more individually and holistically. Less emphasis is placed on standardized test scores and more on the interview, portfolio, recommendations, and essay.

American College Testing (ACT) Program Assessment—An alternative to the SAT, this test has gained wide acceptance by a broad range of institutions in recent years and is given during the school year at test centers. The ACT tests English, mathematics, reading, and science reasoning. These subject test scores can be used in lieu of SAT II subject tests, which are required for admission to some of the more competitive colleges. The score is the average of all four tests; the maximum score is 36.

associate degree—A degree granted by a college or university after the satisfactory completion of a two-year full-time program of study or its part-time equivalent. Types of degrees include the Associate of Arts (A.A.) or Associate of Science (A.S.), usually granted after the equivalent of the first two years of a four-year college curriculum, and the Associate in Applied Science (A.A.S.), awarded upon completion of a technical or vocational program of study.

award package—This is the way colleges and universities deliver their news about student eligibility for financial aid or grants. The most common packages include Pell Grants, Stafford Loans, and Work-Study (see below).

bachelor's or baccalaureate degree—The degree received after the satisfactory completion of a full-time program of study or its part-time equivalent at a college or university. The Bachelor of Arts (B.A.) and the Bachelor of Science (B.S.) are the most common baccalaureates.

branch campus—A campus connected to, or part of, a large institution. Generally, a student spends the first two years at a branch campus and then transfers to the main campus to complete the baccalaureate degree. A branch campus provides a smaller and more personal environment that may help a student mature personally and academically before moving to a larger and more impersonal environment. A branch campus experience may be a good idea for a student who wants to remain close to home or for an adult learner who wishes to work and attend college classes on a part-time basis.

Candidates Reply Date Agreement (CRDA)—If admitted to a college, a student does not have to reply until May 1. This allows time to hear from all the colleges to which the student applied before having to make a commitment to any of them. This is especially important because financial aid packages vary from one school to another, and the CRDA allows time to compare packages before deciding.

college-preparatory subjects—Courses taken in high school that are viewed by colleges and universities as a strong preparation for college work. The specific courses are usually in the five majors areas of English, history, world languages, mathematics, and science. The courses may be regular, honors-level, or AP offerings, and the latter two categories are often weighted when calculated in the GPA.

College Scholarship Service (CSS)—When the federal government changed the FAFSA form several years ago, the College Board created this program to assist postsecondary institutions, state scholarship programs, and other organizations in measuring a family's financial strength and analyzing its ability to contribute to college costs. CSS processes the PROFILE financial form that students may use to apply for non-federal aid. This form is submitted to some 300 private colleges and universities along with the FAFSA when seeking financial aid from these institutions. Participating colleges and universities indicate whether they require this form.

Common and Universal Applications—These college application forms can save students hours of work. The Common Application is presently accepted by about 190 independent colleges, while the Universal is used by about 1,000 schools. The colleges and universities that accept these standardized forms give them equal weight with their own application forms. Students complete the information on the

Game Plan for Getting into College

standardized form and then submit it to any of the schools listed as accepting it. Some schools will return a supplementary form to be completed by the applicant, but most schools base their decisions on these documents alone. The Common Application is available on disk or as a hard copy and can be obtained from your guidance department. The Universal Application is available on the Web.

control—A college or university can be under public or private control. Publicly controlled universities are dependent on state legislatures for their funding, and their policies are set by the agencies that govern them. Private colleges and universities are responsible to a board of directors or trustees. They usually have higher tuition and fees to protect the institutions' endowment.

cooperative education—A college program that alternates between periods of full-time study and full-time employment in a related field. Students are paid for their work and gain practical experience in their major, which helps them apply for positions after graduation. It can take five years to obtain a baccalaureate degree through a co-op program.

cost of education—This includes tuition and fees, room and board, books and supplies, transportation, and miscellaneous expenses. A student's financial aid eligibility is the difference between the cost of education and the Expected Family Contribution as computed by the federal government using the FAFSA.

course load—The number of course credit hours a student takes in each semester. Twelve credit hours is the minimum to be considered a full-time student. The average course load per semester is 16 credit hours.

credit hours—The number of hours per week that courses meet are counted as equivalent credits for financial aid and used to determine your status as a full- or part-time student.

cross-registration—The practice, through agreements between colleges, of permitting students enrolled at one college or university to enroll in courses at another institution without formally applying for admission to the second institution. This can be an advantage for students in a smaller college who might like to expand options or experience another learning environment.

deferred acceptance—The admissions decision is being moved to a later date.

deferred admission—This policy permits students to postpone enrollment for one year after acceptance to a college or university.

double major—Available at most schools, the double major allows a student to complete all the requirements to simultaneously earn a major in two fields.

dual enrollment—This policy allows a student to earn college credit while still in high school. Many of these course credits can be transferred to a degree-granting institution, especially if the student maintains a minimum of a B average. A college, however, may disallow courses taken in the major field of concentration at another institution because its policy dictates that all courses in the major must be taken at the college. When considering dual enrollment, students should talk with the admissions offices at the colleges they are considering enrolling in to make sure that they will accept credit transfers.

Early Action (EA)—A student applies to a school early in the senior year, between October 30 and January 15, and requests an early application review and notification of admission. The answer usually takes three to four weeks after application. If accepted, the student is not obligated to attend that institution but can bank this admission and still apply to other colleges during the regular admission cycle.

early admission—Some colleges will admit certain students who have not completed high school, usually exceptional juniors. The students are enrolled full-time and do not complete their senior year of high school. Colleges usually award high school diplomas to these students after they have completed a certain number of college-level courses.

Early Decision (ED)—Sometimes confused with Early Action, the Early Decision plan allows students to apply to an institution early in the senior year, also between October 30 and January 15, and request an early notification of admission. The student and his guidance counselor sign a contract with the school at the time of application that indicates that if accepted, the student is obligated to attend that institution. Some colleges and universities offer both ED and EA options.

emphasis—An area of concentration within a major or minor; for example, an English major may have an emphasis in creative writing.

Expected Family Contribution (EFC)—The amount of financial support a family is expected to contribute toward a child's college education. This amount is part of the formula used by the federal government to determine financial aid eligibility using the FAFSA form.

external degree program—A program of study whereby a student can earn credit through independent study, college courses, proficiency examinations, distance learning, or personal experience. External degree colleges generally have no campus or classroom facilities. They are sometimes referred to as "colleges without walls."

Federal Pell Grant Program—This is a federally sponsored and administered program that provides grants based on need to under-graduate students. Congress annually sets the appropriation; amounts range from around $400 to $3,000 annually. This is "free" money because it does not need to be repaid.

Federal Perkins Loan Program—This is a federally run program based on need and administered by a college's financial aid office. This program offers low-interest loans for undergraduate study. Repayment does not begin until a student graduates. The maximum loan amount is $3,000 per year.

Federal Stafford Loan—Another federal program based on need that allows a student to borrow money for educational expenses directly from banks and other lending institutions (sometimes from the colleges themselves). These loans may be either subsidized or unsubsidized. Repayment begins six months after a student's course load drops to less than half-time. Currently the interest rate is 0 percent while in school and then is variable up to 8.25 percent. The loan must be repaid within ten years.

Federal Work-Study Program (FSW)—A federally financed program that arranges for students to combine employment and college study. The employment may be an integral part of the academic program (as in cooperative education or internships) or simply a means of paying for college.

Free Application for Federal Student Aid (FAFSA)—This is the federal government's instrument for calculating need-based aid. It is available from high school guidance departments, college financial aid offices, and the Internet (www.fafsa.ed.gov). The form should be completed and mailed as soon after January 2 as possible.

gap—The difference between the amount of a financial aid package and the cost of attending a college or university. The student and her family are expected to fill the gap.

grants/scholarships—These are financial awards that are usually dispensed by the financial aid offices of colleges and universities. The awards may be need- or merit-based. Most are need-based. Merit-based awards may be awarded on the basis of excellence in academics, leadership, volunteerism, athletic ability, or a special talent.

Greek life—This phrase refers to sororities and fraternities. These organizations often have great impact on the campus social life of a college or university.

honors program—Honors programs offer an enriched, top-quality educational experience that often includes small class sizes, custom-designed courses, mentoring, enriched individualized learning, hands-on research, and publishing opportunities. A handpicked faculty guides students through the program. Honors programs are a great way to attend a large school that offers enhanced social and recreational opportunities while receiving an Ivy League-like education at a reduced cost.

independent study—This option allows students to complete some of their credit requirements by studying on their own. A student and his or her faculty adviser agree in advance on the topic and approach of the study program and meet periodically to discuss the student's progress. A final report is handed in for a grade at the end of the term.

interdisciplinary—Faculty members from several disciplines contribute to the development of the course of study and may co-teach the course.

internship—This is an experience-based opportunity, most often scheduled during breaks in the academic calendar, whereby a student receives credit for a supervised work experience related to his major.

major—The concentration of a number of credit hours in a specific subject. Colleges and universities often specify the number of credits needed to receive a major, the sequence of courses, and the level of courses necessary to complete the requirements.

merit awards, merit-based scholarships—More "free" money, these awards are based on excellence in academics, leadership, volunteerism, athletic ability, and other areas determined by the granting organization, which can be a college or university, an organization, or an individual. They are not based on financial need.

minor—An area of concentration with fewer credits than a major. The minor can be related to the major area of concentration or not; for example, an English major may have a minor in theater.

need blind—Admissions decisions made without reference to a student's financial aid request, that is, an applicant's financial need is not known to the committee at the time of decision.

nonmatriculated—A student who has either not been admitted yet but is taking classes or has been academically dismissed. Under this category, a student may neither receive financial aid nor participate in an athletic program at that school.

open admissions—A policy of admission that does not subject applicants to a review of their academic qualifications. Many public junior/community colleges admit students under this guideline, that is, any student with a high school diploma or its equivalent is admitted.

Preliminary Scholastic Assessment Test (PSAT)/National Merit Scholarship Qualifying Test—This test, given in October, duplicates the kinds of questions asked on the SAT but is shorter and takes less time. Usually taken in the junior year, the test also acts as a qualifying instrument for the National Merit Scholarship Awards Program and is helpful for early college guidance.

Reserve Officers' Training Corps (ROTC)—Each branch of the military sponsors an ROTC program. In exchange for a certain number of years on active duty, students can have their college education paid for up to a certain amount by the armed forces.

residency requirement—The term has more than one meaning. It can refer to the fact that a college may require a specific number of courses to be taken on campus to receive a degree from the school, or the phrase can mean the time, by law, that is required for a person to reside in the state to be considered eligible for in-state tuition at one of its public colleges or universities.

retention rate—The number and percentage of students returning for the sophomore year.

rolling admissions—There is no deadline for filing a college application. This concept is used most often by state universities. Responses are received within three to four weeks. If admitted, a student is not required to confirm, in most cases, until May 1. Out-of-state residents applying to state universities should apply as early as possible.

Scholastic Assessment Test (SAT) I: Reasoning Test—Also known as "boards" or "board scores" because the test was developed by the College Board. This test concentrates on verbal and mathematical reasoning abilities and is given throughout the academic year at test centers. The maximum combined score for both sections is 1600.

SAT II Subject Tests—These subject-specific exams are given on the same test dates and in the same centers as the SAT I. More emphasis has been placed on these tests in recent years not only because they are used for admission purposes but also for placement and exemption decisions.

seminar—A class that has a group discussion format rather than a lecture format.

Score Choice—An option available only for SAT II testing, which allows a student to review his or her scores before releasing them to colleges. Students can choose which scores to release.

silent scores—The term is applied to PSAT scores because only the student and his or her guidance counselor see the scores. They are not reported to colleges. It is the "practice without penalty" feature of the test.

standby—If a student registers for an SAT or ACT testing date and there are no seats available, the student may accept a standby position; that is, if a seat becomes available the day of the test, the student will take the test. The student must go to the testing center and wait to see if there is an open seat. A fee is attached to standby.

Student Aid Report (SAR)—Report of the government's review of a student's FAFSA. The SAR is sent to the student and released electronically to the schools that the student listed. The SAR does not supply a real money figure for aid but indicates whether the student is eligible.

student-designed major—Students design their own majors under this policy. It offers students the opportunity to develop nontraditional options not available in the existing catalog of majors.

transfer program—This program is usually found in a two-year college or in a four-year college that offers associate degrees. It allows a student to continue his or her studies in a four-year college by maintaining designated criteria set down at acceptance to the two-year program. It is not necessary to earn an associate degree to transfer.

transfer student—A student who transfers from one college or university to another. Credits applied toward the transfer will be evaluated by the receiving school to determine the number it will accept. Each school sets different policies for transfers, so anyone considering this option should seek guidance.

upper division—This term refers to the junior and senior years of study. Some colleges offer only upper-division study. The lower division must be completed at another institution before entering these programs to earn a bachelor's degree.

virtual visit—This is the use of the Internet to investigate various colleges by looking at their home pages. A student can "tour" the college, ask questions via e-mail, read school newspapers, and explore course offerings and major requirements on line. It is not a substitute for a live visit.

waiver to view recommendations—The form many high schools ask their students to sign by which they agree not to review their teachers' recommendation letters before they are sent to the colleges or universities to which they are applying.

yield—The percentage of accepted students who will enter a college or university in the freshman class. These students have received formal acceptance notices and must respond by May 1 with their intention to enroll. The more competitive the school, the higher the yield percentage.

College Planning Timetable Checklist

Tack this key information list and timetable on your refrigerator or the bulletin board in your room where you will see it frequently. Don't bury it on your desk. Refer to it often, and check off items as you have completed them. Following the timetable will help keep you on target for college.

Key Testing Information:

Your high school code (six-digit number) _____

SAT I/II Test Center Codes

Your high school test center code _____

Second-choice school test center code _____

Third-choice school test center code _____

ACT Test Center Codes

Your high school test center code _____

Second-choice school test center code _____

Third-choice school test center code _____

Checklist

_____ Receive my PSAT score and test booklet, share the results with my parents, and review the test to see where improvement is needed.

_____ Register for the May or June SAT. (deadlines: May_____ June _____)

_____ Register for the SAT II: Subject Tests. (deadline _____)

_____ Register to take AP exams in the following subjects with deadlines: AP_____/Date_____; AP_____/Date_____; AP_____ /Date_____

Continue your testing schedule into your senior year, based on the timetable discussed with your counselor. Deadlines for:

SAT I _____   SAT II _____   ACT _____

_____ Register for the TOEFL, which is applicable for ESOL students who have been in the United States for four years or less. (deadline _____)

_____ Discuss senior-year schedule with my counselor.

_____ Discuss my transcript with my counselor and review the requirements for graduation.

_____ By **April 1 of junior year,** distribute the following: three informal teacher recommendation forms, parent descriptive statement, and peer references.

_____ Follow up to be sure that the informal recommendations, parent statement, and peer references have been completed and returned to my counselor.

_____ Discuss early action or early decision options with my counselor before committing. Early action and early decision applications, as well as certain competitive rolling state school applications (e.g., University of Florida, University of Michigan, University of Wisconsin, and University of North Carolina), must be ready for mailing by **October 1 of senior year.**

_____ **By spring of junior year,** complete a review of college criteria and meet with my counselor to generate a computer print-out of potential colleges.

_____ Share the list of colleges with my parents/guardians and schedule a follow-up meeting with my counselor.

_____ Examine college information resources available in the guidance office and media center.

_____ Over the **summer between junior and senior year,** review the Common or Universal Application, complete the short answers and grid portions, and draft the essays (Personal Statement).

_____ Solicit reactions from an English teacher, parent, counselor, etc., and review and rewrite.

_____ Over the **summer or early fall of senior year,** send for college applications and catalogs.

_____ During the **late spring and summer between junior and senior year,** begin visiting colleges. Refer to the "College Exploration Packet," pages 211–12.

_____ Practice the interview. Read the packet on college interviews and view videotape interviews on file. Refer to the "College Exploration Packet."

_____ **Beginning in early autumn of senior year,** meet with college representatives visiting the high school. Check the guidance office bulletin board and listen to the daily announcements for the schedule of upcoming visits.

_____ Arrange for interviews while on campus for a tour or with an assigned alumnus at home. Send a thank-you note to each college representative.

_____ Make my final list of colleges.

_____ Submit formal recommendations to my teachers.

_____ Complete and mail my applications with fees.

　　_____ College 1

　　_____ College 2

　　_____ College 3

_____ Send my official SAT/ACT scores to the colleges on my final list.

_____ Forward an official copy of my transcript to each of the colleges on my final list by their deadlines.

_____ **As soon as possible after January 1 of senior year,** complete my FAFSA forms and Profiles (if required by private colleges) and any other financial aid forms in my college packets.

IMPORTANT: Meet regularly with my guidance counselor to keep her or him informed of my progress and to receive assistance with the process.

A *College Exploration Packet* or *College Planning Guide* is put together by many guidance departments. These packets contain information collected by experienced guidance counselors to help you organize and negotiate the college selection process. The contents will vary from school to school, but generally the packets contain the following items:

1. *College Planning Timetable* (See pages 207–10.)

2. Your high school transcript

3. Your school's profile

4. General college admissions criteria

5. Articles that describe the college admissions selection process

6. Autobiographical Sketch: a series of questions to prompt self-discovery and identify your strengths. This activity will help you to answer questions that may come up during the interview or on college applications.

7. Senior Information Sheet: form on computer disk or in a paper format. Completing this information will help you to rank activities, list athletic involvement, describe honors, and outline employment in a manner that can be readily transferred to college applications.

8. Rate Yourself: a sample of the ranking sections that appear on some college applications. This information shows you the types of questions to which teachers, guidance counselors, and administrators are often asked to respond.

9. Parent Questionnaire and Descriptive Statement: a form. It allows parents to provide insights, not readily available from other sources, about their son or daughter for the guidance counselor.

10. Peer Reference: a form. Students are asked to select a friend (inside or outside of school) who will provide additional information in an articulate manner to assist the guidance counselor in writing recommendations.

Appendix B

Game Plan for Getting into College

11. Common or Universal Application: a sample application. By completing the sample in advance, you will have gathered the information necessary to complete most applications.

12. Request for Transcript: sample standard guidance department form so that you will know what to fill out when requesting transcripts.

13. Waiver: form to sign and return. Many high schools request that students sign a waiver agreeing not to ask to see recommendations.

14. Blank Informal and Formal Recommendation forms

15. Informal Teacher Recommendation forms for use by the guidance counselor

16. Procedure for Obtaining Formal Teacher Recommendations: information that advises students on how to approach teachers for recommendations and how to select recommendation writers

17. Writing Your College Essay: several articles on essay writing and outlining

18. General Advice on Planning a College Visit

19. Suggestions to the Student for the College Interview

20. College Selection Criteria

21. College List: form

22. Postcards: for use in requesting college applications, catalogs, and financial aid information

23. SAT/ACT applications and test booklets

College Visitation Notes

Appendix C

College Name: _____   Date of Visit: _____

Address: _____

Admission Phone # _____   E-mail _____

Likes:	Dislikes:
_____	_____
_____	_____
_____	_____
_____	_____
_____	_____
_____	_____

Score (1–5, 5 being highest)

- Academic Offerings: _____
  How is the curriculum structured?
  What are the strongest programs?
  Are there rigid requirements?
  How strong are the offerings in my field of interest?
- Campus Facilities: _____
  What is the appearance? Modern and accessible?
  What facilities are maintained well? Are they important to you?
- Location: _____
  Is it close to home?
  Is it easily accessible by public transportation?

Game Plan for Getting into College

- Social Life: _____
  What is the overall social environment?
  Does it tend to be Greek? Centered on athletics?
  Intellectually and culturally alive?
- Student Body: _____
  What impression do I have of the students to whom I talked?
  Are they outgoing and friendly? Elitist and snobby? Artsy? Jocks?
  Techies?

Total: _____

My overall impression is:

_____

Information still needed and whom to contact for it:

Information   Contact name and department

_____   _____

_____   _____

_____   _____

A Sample Request for Information From Colleges

Appendix D

[Insert your name]

[Insert Street Address, Town/City, State, Zip]

[Today's Date]

[Name of Admissions Office contact, title]
[School Name]
[City, State or Province, Postal Code]

Dear Mr./Ms. (depends on who contact is):

I am very interested in attending your school beginning in [insert month/year you want to start]. Please send me the following information and any other information that you think would be advisable for me to have:
[Insert here what you still need from this school; possible items are:]

- Application form
- Catalog
- Financial aid information
- School newspaper

My intended major is [insert field of interest]. I attend [insert high school name] in [insert city and state].

My social security number is [insert number].
Thank you for your assistance.

Sincerely,

[Signature]

[Type your name]

The College Search Computer Worksheet

Name: _____ Due Date: _____

What type of school are you interested in?

_____ University   _____ Liberal arts college

_____ Junior/community college   _____ Fine arts college

_____ Technical school/institute   _____ Business college

_____ Other (explain)

_____

_____ Public school   _____ Private school

_____ Either

Location (check one or more)

_____ New England   _____ In-State Only

_____ South   _____ Other Countries

_____ West Coast   _____ Suburban

_____ Mid-Atlantic   _____ Local schools only

_____ Midwest   _____ Urban

_____ Great Lakes states   _____ Rural

Campus Size (number of students)   **Religious Affiliation**

_____ Less than 1,000   _____ Jewish

_____ Between 1,000 and 3,000   _____ Protestant

_____ Between 3,001 and 7,000   (Denomination: _____)

_____ Between 7,001 and 12,000   _____ Roman Catholic

_____ Between 12,001 and 17,000   _____ Other

_____ Above 17,000   _____ Not a Consideration

Appendix E

Characteristics

_____ All women   _____ Coed   _____ All men

What possible majors are you considering?

_____

_____

_____

What possible careers are you interested in?

_____

_____

_____

PSAT Scores: Math _____ Verbal _____ SAT (1st) _____ SAT (2nd) _____

Please list any special interests that you might wish to pursue in college.

Activities

_____

_____

Sports (Indicate Division I, II, or III or intramural.)

_____

_____

Fraternities/Sororities

_____

_____

Accelerated program (i.e., 7-year M.D. program)

_____

_____

Do you have any financial concerns? Y/N   _____

If you are applying as a legacy candidate, please indicate the name of the school, the name of the relative (mother, father, sister, brother) that attended the school, and the years attended:

_____

_____

If there are any specific colleges or universities for which you would like available computer information, please list them below.

1. _____   2. _____

3. _____   4. _____

5. _____   6. _____

Residence Facilities (if applicable)

____ Coed housing   ____ Single-sex housing   ____ No preference

Biography

Patricia Aviezer has spent more than twenty-two years in the field of education as a nurse, teacher, and guidance counselor. The former Chair of the Guidance Department of Edgemont Union Free School District in Scarsdale, New York, she currently serves as Chair of Career and College Counseling at Lake Worth High School in Lake Worth, Florida, where she is spearheading efforts to establish a new school-to-work initiative.

Mrs. Aviezer holds a B.S. from the College of White Plains, an R.N. from the Beth Israel School of Nursing, and an M.S. in education–guidance and counseling from H. H. Lehman College of CUNY. She has served on the Board of Directors for the Westchester, Putnam, and Rockland Counselors Association and is a member of the National Association of College Admissions Counselors (NACAC).

Give Your Admissions Essay An Edge At...

EssayEdge.com

Put Harvard-Educated Editors To Work For You

As the largest and most critically acclaimed admissions essay service, EssayEdge.com has assisted countless college, graduate, business, law, and medical program applicants gain acceptance to their first choice schools. With more than 250 Harvard-educated editors on staff, EssayEdge.com provides superior editing and admissions consulting, giving you an edge over hundreds of applicants with comparable academic credentials.

Visit **www.essayedge.com today,** and take your admissions essay to a new level.

"One of the Best Essay Services on the Internet"
—*The Washington Post*

"The World's Premier Application Essay Editing Service"
—*The New York Times Learning Network*

THOMSON

PETERSON'S

Your everything education destination...
the *all-new* Petersons.com

When education is the question, **Petersons.com** is the answer. Log on today and discover what the *all-new* Petersons.com can do for you. Find the ideal college or grad school, take an online practice admission test, or explore financial aid options—all from a name you know and trust, Peterson's.

www.petersons.com

THOMSON
PETERSON'S ™